Tasting the Dark
New and Selected Poems

Tasting the Dark

New and Selected Poems

George Amabile

The Muses' Company

The Muses' Company Series Editor: Catherine Hunter
Cover design by Doowah Design Inc.
Cover image is "River Park," oil on canvas, 1992, 64" (W) x 72" (H) by William Pura
Author photo by Gordon MacKenzie
Printed and bound in Canada

We acknowledge the financial support of the Manitoba Arts Council and The Canada Council for the Arts for our publishing program.

Canadian Cataloguing in Publication Data

Amabile, George, 1936-
    Tasting the dark: new and selected poems

ISBN 1-896239-66-8

    I. Title.

PS8551.M32T38 2001   C811'.54   C2001-900247-5
PR9199.3.A53T38 2001

Acknowledgements

Many of these poems have been published in the following books, anthologies, journals, magazines and periodicals:

American Goat, Arc, Arts Manitoba, Ariel, Aspen Grove, Blood Ties (Sono Nis Press: Vancouver, 1972), *Border Crossings, Canadian Literature, Caprice, Choice, CVII, Contemporary Poetry of British Columbia* (Sono Nis Press: Vancouver, 1970), *Decal* (Wales), *Descant, Event, The Fiddlehead, Five-O'Clock Shadows* (Letters Bookshop: Toronto, 1996), *Flower and Song* (Borealis Press: Ottawa, 1977), *For Neruda, For Chile* (Beacon Press: Boston, 1975), *Garden Varieties* (Cormorant Books: Dunvegan, 1988), *Grain, The Globe and Mail, Harper's, Ideas of Shelter* (Turnstone Press: Winnipeg, 1981), *Inscriptions* (Turnstone Press: Winnipeg, 1993), *Italian-Canadian Voices* (Mosaic Press: Montreal, 1984), *L'Altra Storia* (Monteleone: Vibo Valentia, 1998); *The Literary Review of Canada, Margin* (England), *Matrix, Modern Poetry Studies, The Moosehead Review, The New American Poets* (Follett: Chicago, 1968), *New Mexico Quarterly, The New Quarterly, The New Yorker Book of Poems* (The Viking Press: New York, 1970), *Open Country* (Turnstone Press: Winnipeg, 1976), *Origins, Out of Place* (Coteau Books: Regina, 1991), *The Pacific Quarterly Moana* (New Zealand), *The Penguin Book of Canadian Verse* (Penguin Books: Markham, 1975), *The Pittsburgh Quarterly, Poetry Canada Review, Poet's Gallery, The Poets of Canada* (Hurtig: Edmonton, 1973), *Prairie Fire, The Presence of Fire* (McClelland and Stewart: Toronto, 1982), *Prism International, Quarry, Rumours of Paradise /Rumours of War* (McClelland and Stewart: Toronto, 1995), *Section Lines: A Manitoba Anthology* (Turnstone Press: Winnipeg, 1988), *Sur* (Buenos Aires), *The Tamarack Review, Undozen* (Black Moss Press: Windsor, 1982), *Waves,* and *Writers' News Manitoba.*

"Snow," "She Drives Back, in a Bad Mood, after a Party," "*Tivoli: The Villa D' Este,*" "The Sun Shower," "Oranges," "Networks," "From a Journal," "The Whirlpool" and "Freeze" were first published, some in substantially different versions, by *The New Yorker.*

"Tasting the Dark" and "Nouvelle Cuisine" first appeared in *Saturday Night*.

"Popular Crime" won first prize in the Sidney Booktown International Poetry Contest.

I am grateful to The Canada Council for the Arts and the Manitoba Arts Council for their continued support.

I would like to thank Arthur Adamson, David Arnason, Jim Keller, Mhari Mackintosh, George Payerle, Kevin Roberts, and Carol Shields, who gave their time and intelligence to the onerous task of reading previous books and recommending poems for inclusion in this one.

Finally, I am indebted to my editor, Catherine Hunter, whose extraordinary readership, illuminating commentary and sustained enthusiasm have given the book its present shape and character.

Table of Contents

Blood Ties

Accidental Death
(Anthony Amabile Jr., 1938-1951)

1

It was late
morning. August
woodflies, drawn by the flushed
acceleration of blood
whirred around our heads
like a halo of atoms
as we jounced over craters
of stony road. I struggled
with his broken-geared bike,
gripping the handlebar
till the knuckles I'd skinned
trying to fix it burned, but he
let loose a cowboy holler
standing tall
in the saddle of my new Schwinn.

An already half-broken promise
to a pair of ginger twins
was making me nervous. I shouted
STAY BEHIND ME, DAMMIT
when he tried to pass
leaning like a racer into the wind.

2

Skidding and braking
along the highway's gravelled shoulder
I heard the pow of a burst tire,
the rattle of a dump truck...
I turned and caught a splitsecond glimpse
of chrome handles raking the air
like horns at a sick angle
bright bashed spokes

milky smoke that clung to the black
smear his wheels had rubbed on the roadway.

I was in the air
when his body slammed
into the grass and rolled
up in a heap. I landed
running, tearing
his name loose from the press
of terror that had stopped my breath.
I knelt and rocked
him senseless in my lap.

      3

My mother's face in a grey
doorway, pretty and kind
until it caved in like a wet
hillside of flowers.

I let my eyes cruise
a field of corn
papery leaves
crackling in the wind.
If I squinted I could see
trucks on the highway miles away
smaller than toys.

      4

I crossed a board bridge
on wobbly legs
over dead water choked
with scum, and walked
toward the sheds
under a breathless overlay
of shadows, trees: sun
at the still height of summer
wild grapes ripening

under a loosely shingled roof
of leaves. Grass
furled away from the path
like ploughed hair.

5

Squawking chickens
raised ammonia clouds
that clawed my throat
and seared my nostrils.
His after-school hermitage
of beasts was thick
with gloom. When I tried
to feed his rabbits
they pressed against the back
wall of their cage, trembling.
A wasp came out of the shadows,
came so close it filled the shed
with a furious blur of wings.

6

Tarpaper and white paint
blistered on the door
of the outhouse. The brass knob
I had puckered with bulletholes
teaching him how to draw
a bead burned in my palm.
I shut out the sun to think
He's dead. I'm glad
it wasn't me. I watched
a pair of houseflies collide
and lock in a buzz of lust.

Alarmed by rabbits
he'd barged into my room, yelling
"The big one's on top of the small one.
He's biting and he won't stop."

But his eyes opened, clear
as wells when I told him
how it was....

7

All day I could not touch
his death. I saw him waking
in some other, dazzling
afternoon, brushing off grass
a stranger armed
with lightness and a grin.

But when I closed my fingers
around the sculpted heap of cold
hands in the coffin
vision drained into the ground.

Snow

Basic White

Angels
might fall that way
out of their myth-
ical, bloodless war
into the dark
street's electric light.

Stilled syllables
flakes
locked in the dead heat
of that debate
steer a dazed, formal dance
through cold halos.

The Shadows

Driving straight roads
at night, I flinch
inside as the blurred arrows
die into the windshield:
white poisonous thoughts:
tracer bullets hurled from the last war.

No. This is a delicate
invasion. Drops
that have grown so cold
they flower cling
to the blind shapes of this world.

Station Break

In the dark bedroom
a girl shrugs off
her mohair sweater.

What is this shocked
blue crackling
if not some abstract god
who cares, desperately
for the shape and feel
of her human shoulders?

Static.
A cold fact.

News of the World

The snow is cold, factual, a mind
battering static that proliferates
at windows and litters my T.V. screen
with dandruff, heroin
flaked ash from the ovens of the Third Reich...

Angels.
Pale Barbarians.
This is the white plague.
Sugary insect faces
continue to fall
into the eyes of lit cities
out of the dark ages of the sky.

She Drives Back, in a Bad Mood, after a Party

In shades of whiskied sleep
I watch her features turn to soft
iron, her hair to fog. She drifts
away from me...away.
My feelings poke around in some old slag heap
until the light of day
filters in to lead me back.

Last week we watched the harbour's ice-field crack.
Great slabs tilted and slipped, rose
like a time-lapse mountain range.
The next day, water cradled a sleek parade:
figures of people and animals, turning
in a sarabande of glistening dissolution.
Even the dust sang a small song.

Her face has changed. The early light
builds faint lustres in her hair and the slight
smile she offers breaks
into all the sun I need.
Shadows contract. The sun outside
hammers a lead-grey sea into gold flakes.

Tivoli: The Villa D' Este

The body dies; the body's beauty lives.
            —Wallace Stevens

The fountains glistened with sound as the wind rose.
Hadrian watched a waterjet trying to keep
its willowy shape intact in a storm of rainbows
and saw Aphrodite, crowned with foam, deep

in the mind.
                    Ruins.
                            How many shrines, stars,
empires have fallen since then? A second wind
sweeps the reflective pool to chipped marble
but the stone girls of *Karyai* stand, sustained

by what? Folds of soaked fine-woven cloth
are pressed flat, still, against thigh and nipple
by imagined weather, desire eased *out of thought*
and found again under the powdering tip

of a chisel. It blows where I stand, *has* blown
for thousands of years, in the flesh, between water and stone.

The Sun Shower

…Miracles occur
If you care to call those spasmodic
Tricks of radiance miracles.
　　　—Sylvia Plath

Down the street
a Sunday of empty parks.

I watch myself
slide by
mirrors and shop windows.

Clouds assemble, grey
stones in a wall. All morning
the light has been thickening
toward rain. Now
the river's blown
ripple-patterns
grow suddenly still
and it begins, drowsy
as hemlock, a chill
drizzle that packs me in
-to a doorway's upright box.

Spidery limbs crawl
over the blank numbered faces
of clocks behind my face
which hangs, a ghost
about to evaporate
in the glass
between this universe
of concealed springs,
gears that whirr with insect speech
and a town wiped out by rain.

Inklings breathe
at the back of my mind

like the unshelled bodies of snails
and there's a shift
from the mouselight of self-hypnosis
to long spattering bursts
of relief. The overcast
breaks up like an ice field in April
and wherever sunlight lights the bouncing rain
on the sleek tar, on the rinsed roofs
and hoods and bumpers of cars
even on flat water
it surprises thousands
of horned creatures the colour of glass
whose looked-through lives become visible
only when they have something to dance about.

Oranges

Afternoons in Connecticut
we'd picnic by the lake
on a Mexican sarape:
primary colours
expanding in raw wool
under a still life: chicken,
apples, a bottle of *Chablis*…

This morning, having lived
for weeks on dollars a day—
ripped newspaper on a string in the bathroom
straw mattress on the bed—we discover
breakfast: oranges, opened
at the window in Greek light.

Their juice bursts in the mouth
like the sun on closed eyelids
like the whole fire that writhes
at the centre of systems, scattering
tiger lilies among bleached ruins
like the pulse that flickered for Aeschylus
in the slow dawn of the Oresteia
or the twist of flaming wind
carried by runners from ancient cities
to the new Olympic Stadium
in Rome, east
to west as Apollo rides the sky
over dead leaves in New England
toward the dark.
                    But first
the thin skin of an orange
flame, filmed
by still water breaks
into bull's-eye ripples
as the bream come up to feed.

Networks

Traffic starts
and stops, locked
in a grid of right
angles. As the lights
change, invisible
barricades lift and fall.

This is an old idea.

Off the coast, all day,
green nylon
webbing rustles
as the gill net opens
like a fan from its creaking drum
and sinks into the skiff's wake
thin as the wing of an insect
between the lead-line
and the string of puffed-rice corks.

Suspended in seadrift
it disappears but stays.
Keeping it straight
in a running tide
takes more than patience
or the rack
of charts that collect
dust on the cabin ceiling.

Through the long afternoons
voices of other fishermen
not saying much
crackle around a loose connection.

At dark set
the constellations wheel overhead,
tuned by lines of force.
Who knows, for sure, where the fish are?

Open Country

From a Journal

I'd been off by myself trying to evolve.
It had to be done
in the dark
under tight security.
I chose this northern lake
the auroras turning at night like lucid scarves
the afternoons of lime-green snow.

I remember the taste of fish eggs
on rice in sub-zero weather
the smell of cold fur
slow frost in firelight
given the run of the cabin
and the wolves
who were starving in their deep twilights.

Once I saw
(or was it merely hunger)
the blooming of nebulae
radiant colours
the sudden coherence like a sun
haze burning off
then a star cluster
and a pinwheel of dust
six billion miles from rim to rim.

And that was all.
Though the mind was willing
the body thinned
out like breath in a blizzard.
By the time they found me I was a changed man.

Prairie

a light word
sun spokes through the overcast
at dusk, or smoke
totems wisping away
into beige emulsions

an earth word
a moist darkness turning
stones and roots
fossils and tiny lives
up to the sky

a watery word
mirage and heat lightning
steadied by pewter barns
where whole towns float in a lilting haze
and rumours of rain rise from the chartreuse lakes

a flame-shaped word
a ragged mane blowing
for miles across dry fields
lighting the night
like the campfires of a vast migration

a word with *air*
in its belly that howls
for hours or days and dries
the memory of soft conversation
to wheatdust under the tongue.

The Whirlpool

Yellow or blue
cataract/waterfall
appleandrose
turn slowly in this wind
-less high as the smoke
rises and the day hangs
fire in green leaves

I unlock a drawer
in the musty bedroom
of an abandoned cottage

Books, records, a silver flask
and the scattered photographs
of those who lived here before the war
disintegrate in a burst of light

The grain of the woodwork flows out
into the room which darkens
like an old movie & drifts
off, into a shy corner
                    of the forest

Waves gleam on the beach
A rainbow blur, lake water
tangled in dark lashes,
echoes and echoes over the stones

Flower and Song

everyday gods

each afternoon at three
like tons of galloping milk
above the sea, thunder
-heads with the faces
of immortal toads
gather and clothe
in shadow the town's adobe
blaze, chill
the air, and cool
raindrops pelt the streets,
explode into dust
-covered roe, collect
in quivering beanshapes
that run together till the dust
is gone and the stones
gleam (amethyst and coral)
under a wrinkling sheet
of water that churrs
like a river but dries to a hush
of broad leaves in the sun
long before bells
for *visperas* wake
the valley with bronze echos
and long before it's time
for *Doña Elena*
to carry the pail of live coals
up to her taco stand in the *jardín*
or for the keen breath of the mountain
to raise, from that black pod
a serpent shape
feathered with fiery seeds
against the ice-blue armies
of the night

Manolo Martinez
for John Logan

We sit in the cave of Los Dragones
under the six-guns, machetes and hurricane lamps
that hang like hard fruit from shadowy rafters
tequila hangovers rocked by street glare
and the bright clothes of strollers.

Over the slip and scrape
of spiked heels on illogical stones
a petulant female voice complains
"But what is there to *do* here?"
John's boozy basso profundo booms
from the dark bar's giant megaphone
"Why doan ju go to thee bullfight in Querétaro?"
The young man scowls and the woman brightens
but they move on, past the blazing doorway.

We leave our table and enter the day's arena.
John leans on his hand-polished cane
while I haggle with a cabbie
who will speed us with his demon smile over melting roads.

In Querétaro we troop with the crowd
up a ramp toward the hot blue sky.
The police feel us out from armpits to shoetops
and hand us red bandanas that say *Martinez.*

High in the stands on seats of stained cement
we drink beer from waxed cups
watching the afternoon sun glow
through paper into a storm of gold motes
till *pasodoble* trumpets
ream small-talk from the *plaza*
and scour the remaining silence clean.

When the killer of bulls appears with his train of *peónes*
cheers and shouts, flowers and hats
sail down toward his arms raised in salute.

He walks three times around the ring
erect and proud, a cape
draped over his arm, the heels of his boots
leaving a trail of prints in the brushed sand.

Under the stands a rusty gate opens
and a half ton of furious meat with horns
gallops across the packed arena
thuds the *barrera*
bounces back and sits on his tail.

He shakes his head, looks up at the wreath
of tiered faces. TORO we shout, ÉJE, TORO.
The *picador* trots out on a starved nag.
He looks like a grim Quixote, thin
legs gripping the padded quilt
that cannot shield the triphammer heart,
the soft belly, the heaving ribs
of the horse whose eyes are wild
as he rears and sidesteps, huge
black cock unfolding, shooting
a torrent of hot piss at the sand.

The sharp knife at the end of the lance
nuzzles the sleek hump and works itself in
till the bull stands up, forcing
the slender wooden shaft into a bow
that splits and splinters. He lowers his head
drives his horns, again and again
up under the useless quilt which tears
loose as he turns and the dazed horse backs
off, stumbling over the knot of its own intestines.

Attendants flash the pink insides
of their capes at the bull who paws
the earth, gathers a dark
intent that explodes into a gallop.
When flamingo satin flares, he skids
to a stop and hooks
a blast of empty air.
          OLÉ

Elegant costumes glitter and prance
around the black beast who charges
and turns, charges and turns, then stands
snorting, heaving his head at the sky.

Martinez waves the *toreros* off
and strolls into the silence of ten thousand eyes.
He smiles at the bull,
breaks two *banderillas* over his knee,
      OLÉ

then his arms go out and up and he stands on his toes
wrists bent in, pointing
the snapped frilly darts at the bull's hump.
He starts to run, a sidewinding dance
of short, quick steps, pulls
in his hips as the horns cut by
and stabs both barbed tips into bunched muscle.
          OLÉ

He struts to the *barrera*
wipes his face with a white towel
comes back and does it again.
      OLÉ
And again.
      OLÉ
Six short ribboned sticks
flop from the bull's back.

Martinez unfolds his cape and begins to work.

A *serpentina, veronicas,* the pass
of death on his knees with his back
to the bull, so close we can hear
the horn scrape
against his gold brocade.

He calls for the sword and *muleta.*
The silence of the crowd deepens.
A cloud passes briefly over the sun.

He taps both horns with the flexible tip of his weapon
and the small sound it makes grows in the breeze.

The beast's insulted rage heaves
his drained heart into one last charge
as Martinez leaves his feet and leans
on the curved blade that sinks between shuddering bones.
Blood wells up and spills from the black hide.
The bull drops to his knees and the man steps free.

We stamp and clap.
A single deafening voice chants
   MANOLO, MANOLO, MATADOR
   MANOLO, MANOLO, TORERO.

Machete

Jim sets up
his latest painting against
a chair. The oils
are still wet. He laughs,
"It's colourful, but
what the hell is it?"

Willowy ochre leaves
flattened by a blast
of saffron
        wind
above a grey-white
blur, two vertical streaks
of purple and a silver
strip that barely turns
up at the tip.

"I see a man in wine-
coloured pants, nearly
erased by mist," I tell him,
"standing in this
field, cutting
        sugarcane…"

He goes to work, trimming
the grey a bit, tightening
that drift of morning
smoke to the folds of a shirt. Liquid
white freshens the sweep
of a hat brim. He leans
back, studies it for a while
then turns it over and writes
Machete
Goese/Amabile, 1968.

Canto
to Pablo Neruda

Musician of stern autumns and whispering steel
maestro of the mind's muscle
your violent flowers and fragile storms invade us
like the miracles of an affectionate technology

Sure
even in darkness
you walk the desolate coast
your ancient head silvered by moonlight
and battered by invisible capes of the wind

You are crooning to the surrounding night
in a clean voice full of surprises
the shy loves of weeds and lichen
boots tomatoes and salt

On the far shore
men still shovel coal & dusty ore in the red ghost-light of the mills
Their sweat shines like the oil of your poems
Women spread their wrinkled wash over shrubs in the early sun
They are lean and strong and quick of tongue
And children run barefoot through the shadows of century plants
Their laughter cracks open and spills in the wind

Ideas of Shelter

First Kill

1

I always wanted
to be a great

white hunter.
It wasn't easy

crawling
over the hot roof

of the toolshed
dragging my Daisy

carbine, peering
down into the cinders

and grass of the alley
till the big, striped

tabby made its move.
Bee-bees rattled

as I lowered my sights.
The smell of machine oil

stoned me. *Pffft.*
Direct hit. But the beast

yowled, spit
back and vamoosed.

2

An accident taught me
how to draw blood.

41

We were playing
in a lot with broken glass.

Who could throw
the fragments higher.

I winged one out of sight.
It returned, buzzing,

and cut the muscle
of Anthony Morga's calf.

3

They're up there
tucked away in struts
and shadows of the trestle

cooing and dropping
spatterdung on the street.
I watch them creep

out and rise
with a flurry of wing noise
wheeling in broken arcs

over the city. But
before they leave
their dingy labyrinth

they stop to puff
their chest feathers
and cock their heads.

That's when I pull
the inner tube
strips tight. Reee*lease*.

The bottle chip spins, hissing
cutting its take-off
to a floppy dive. He hits

the sidewalk and sits
there, one wing
flailing the kerb.

I pick him up.
He bleeds into my hands.

      4

When the cops pass, I edge
into the alley and run
two blocks to a loose board
in the coal-yard fence.

I can feel his normal fever
against my skin. Why
won't he die? I toss him back
into the air but he can't

fly. When I lift him
again, one eye stares
vacant as garnet. Though his heart
races, he makes no move

to escape. I could leave him
for the cats, or keep him
a secret in my room, but that's
for kids and sisters. This

is where the gang made me
smoke, drink gin and scratch
its name on my arm, where I jumped
without clothes for a lousy buck

from the railroad bridge into a pile
of pea coal. No one's here.
I've got that choked feeling
you get the first time

you steal, or buy dirty books.
I've watched my father do it,
in the yard, with chickens:
Loop the string over scaly feet

and hoist them up. Then you squeeze
the beak wide, feed
the blade into his throat and cut.
Shudders. Violent wings.

Blood like royal vomit. Warm
feathers come loose with the sound
of ripped stitches. They're still
in the air when I slit

the skin, gut him, cut
off the head, the feet, then push
a stick through the body
and hold it

over a flaming nest
of brown paper bags and stained newspaper.

     5

Without salt, without
water to wash

his death away the taste
was wild, but I chewed
and swallowed even the small wishbone.

Totem: Black Bear

Dreamt smells under the snow
decay. The darkness heaves.
A wall of spoiled ice
collapses. Then
cave-draught, glare
and hunger beating up from the pit.

Spring is a blur. Smudged
trees, the wind soaked with flora
and a trace of musk that grows
grows, over pounding turf
till bracken crackles
and a lithe panic breaks for home.

Hugged. Broken. Jaws
close on the slack
neck, the sweet
reek of blood…

Each time the chase takes
longer. There are days
when nothing moves but the air
the water, and rage
fades into summer.

Berries, nuts, wild honey—
it is impossible to remember
breath raw in the lungs
the white silence. But it will come,
a soft bulk over the muscles
under a hardening breeze, the cold,
the drugged search for a bed that fits like a grave.

Point of Balance
to Susan Musgrave

The gulls come in
out of the calm
greys of a layered sky.

It is almost evening.
You are standing in your thin bones
graceful and irreducible
among the rocks, your hands
your fingers, combing the willowy shallows
of ash-blond hair, your eyes
widening carefully in the dusk.

It's your way of escaping
words and the craft of words
if only to let them surprise you
as you sail out into grey rifts
and glide skilfully back.

It's darker now.
The gulls turn above you
dropping their throaty cries
into your silence. They will not touch
your shoulders, will not even brush
your hair with their wings
but they seem aware
in the poised light before nightfall
that you ride the same wind.

Wherever the world
invites you, you will arrive
out of this feathery distance
with absolute eyes, and a smile
like wings adjusting the sky at the edge of water.

En Passant

When the time comes, time
slips and your voice goes on
reaching in the damp night. It slows
because your words are trying to find
The Moment of Truth, a ruse
we both see through, in the dark, toes
stretching toward stars from the confined
flight of playground swings, as taxis grind
out their obscure missions. Kiss.
Embrace. Good Bye. I know I'll miss
this: delicate shade of mind
on mind, openings, knots that unwind
in the fine tuning after years
of friendship, as the air between us clears.

How often can this happen? Is it known
for sure, in the dusty labyrinths, that we only
find it once, this fullness, this levelling out?
That afternoon in the wind, your mouth
smiled above the wrecked, brown
imitation shale New York becomes
from its highest roofs. We looked down
across the gleam of water, into the numb
climates of junk that spawned us. Then
you had to get back, to your office
your job. I wondered when
I would see you, after that awkward kiss.
You sounded unhappy, distant, arch on the phone.
Did you know I could love you and leave you alone?

Christmas week. I climb out of bed,
pad, unsteady with flu, down
to the mailbox. Brass. The dead
face of brass opens. Bills. Town
Houses, Condominiums, Crown

Land For Sale this once. We are fed
such ignorant come-ons. But the sound
of your voice, wind in the trees,
days I left like a green shore
are there too when I read
"Please forgive the mood I was in…" I tore
the ticket home in half in my head
but what could I say, if I'd knocked at your door
(after midnight) that hadn't been said?

I stand in the shabby hallway, in the noon
light, high on your promise, "Next time…"
I could drop a thin dime
in the payphone, wait through clicks
and hope that your morning would take
my voice in stride, out of the sticks,
out of a past your card and your note rake
and fan to a small flame with their seasonal gift
of words: "Thanks for your visit." Shall I croon
to you? Shall I tell you the lift
of that evening sails like a full moon
over the city's competitive bricks?
If I did that, something might break.

So I climb back to my room and start a letter.
"Glad you wrote. I like your 'beingness' too."
In the silence, I watch her fold a sweater
arrange weed/flowers in a blue
jar. Traffic. Snow. "When I'm with you
time deepens and clears. It was hard
leaving. You must have felt I didn't want to."
I remember the easy fit of her arms,
the way we talked about takers and givers
on the hood of someone's polished car
and the tide that ebbed when I turned into the river
wind, caught a cab, a plane. "Though the star
that governs this connection thins,
my sense of you, your sense of me, brightens."

Oil Rig

Just off shore
it nods like a pop-art donkey
pumping the expensive blood of eons
into holding tanks that never hold enough.

It's awkward and ingenious
like the twentieth-century mind.
It spoils the view
but works non-stop while we sleep.

It's a metronome,
squeaky, dead to the world,
and there are those who say
one day people will fit that way

into the march of time.
But I hear Fyodor Dostoyevsky
muttering under the ground,
I am a man and not a piano key.

from Blue Denim

1. The Investiture

Once it was the cloth
of sails, opening
surly chapters in this hemisphere.

Now, drenched with indigo
stiff as a new idea
my factory-tailored uniform creaks
and chafes, against the landlocked
rhythms of thigh and shoulder.

Pulling it on, each morning
it's easier to cast off
into the day's adventures.
After months of wind
sun, sweat, the push
of muscle, whirlpools of hot soap
cocktail parties, concert halls and fairs
it will ride softly
worn to the bone-
white thread, the wise
blue of cleared horizons.

2. Meditation over a Rusty Oil Drum

How much does anyone really need?
Love, food, shelter, a game
or two to pass the time...

This is a beginning, burning
the complex wardrobes that disguise
how deeply we share these
inhuman conditions, sentenced
to death for having been born
though we were never consulted

and did not agree. *New clothes*
upon new sticks. But the shadows
that glide down from the storm
are the same. And *there's more enterprise*
in the clear eye, the balanced mind, the body's carriage.

3. Class

A tallish man in a sharp suit and a brand new sheepskin coat
stands near the elevator on the top floor of a government building.
He pulls the luxurious collar up and struts back and forth.
It is obvious that he's in a good mood and proud of his clothes.

At the far end of the hall a glass door opens.
A figure in a fifteen-dollar khaki parka, jeans
and a hat of dyed rabbit fur comes through.
He is preoccupied with the chore this errand has handed his life
but he looks up in time to see the tanned face turn away smirking.
Something rises inside him. He watches the hunched, elegant back
the abrupt swagger, the jounce of barbered curls under snap-brimmed suede
until the pacing sir turns back, grinning contemptuously down
at the shorter man's ridiculous costume
and their eyes meet.
                    It is obvious that the magazine ad
expects the dark, probably foreign, army/navy foam-filled winter twill
to drop his gaze and look away, but he doesn't.
He stares back, eyes lit, mouth composed, his stride unchecked
and the other flusters, remembering bad teeth
or the cold sore under his Buffalo Bill moustache.
His Acapulco tan goes a shade greyer.
He looks around nervously, sees they're alone
and steps aside to let the shit-for-clothes perhaps assassin
enter the smooth doors which have just opened
but the trim, lithe, nondescript nobody smiles, glides
to the right, keeps moving, pushes
through an exit door
and jogs out of sight down seventeen flights of marble.

5. Brand

Once upon a time, a furred fist
pulled a half-burnt branch from the fire.
Its glowcoal eye wheeled
smoking through the moonlight.
Something fierce turned
and fled.
        Now it's not even hot
iron singeing a bristly hide
but a clever mistake like *Treet*
stuck on cans of homogenized meat
or the outright lie, *New Freedom*:
pads of compressed cotton
"especially designed to make you feel
like the kind of a woman...."
whose vulva drips wild honey when aroused.

9. The Conversion of Professor Pease

Yes, I've been known to imbibe
from time to time
but that has nothing to do
with this. It began a month ago.
I was eating a piece of whole wheat toast
when snow outside the window
melted into a field of grain
blown toward the west
and sprinkled with small birds.
Herds of Black Angus lowed when I chewed
the steak, and the first mouthful of eggs
showed me a dozen hens
pecking among stones and tentpegs
near a creek. Of course it was a trick
of the mind, but I was intrigued.
I'd wait for popcorn
to change elephants on the movie screen
into silk tassels, leaves that clacked in the breeze.

Torn between exhilaration
and fear, I told no one. Instead
I pared my lifestyle down to the bone:
two rooms, one typewriter, one guitar
a good view of the north star
pragmatic arguments *ad infinitum*
and work shirts of blue denim
worn beyond distinctions of class
that say, "This is what I want to be:
human, durable, self-supporting and free.
I'll pay my dues if you'll get off my ass."

10. Homestead

Fire pours
a sound like the wind in small leaves
through the shapes of a river
into a fierce blue sky.

The cold is behind us
like a broken bottle.

We turn back into it every day
gathering dead branches
as weather tightens around the sun
and the air fills with crystals.

By spring I'll understand:
the map in the palm of my hand
has led me to this hill of old failures.

The axe falls, the tree
falls, night falls and water
goes on smoking into the gorge.
But nature won't wash
our dirty laundry. Sure
there's plenty of room
but even here the air's not clear
and a light rain will tarnish the hardiest bloom.

12. Critical Mass

After a million years
as populations mushroom
we celebrate an odd communion:
the sum of human genius
and ignorance fused
in a flash, ten thousand suns
unfolding dense cloud
out of itself on the horizon.

> *Dimpled buttocks, the swollen*
> *shallows behind your knees.*
> *From these pools, peace*
> *enters my tongue, my brain, my bloodstream*
> *in silver slips that explode*
> *inside, damaging no one.*

War can't be outlawed
because it's what happens
among consenting adults.
The madmen of history
could never have pulled their expensive stunts
without us. We're proud of that.
We preserve their names, their faces,
their bloody deeds in books, in stone
as though brain damage in high places
were evidence of superhuman light.

Because it's easier
for men like Xerxes or Idi Amin
to convince millions that they have earned
the blind faith of absolute rule
by passing through the asshole of a camel
than it is for a single mind to keep itself whole.

What is it, gentlemen,
this chain of command?
Can we shake it?
Can we play with it like a kitten?
Can we wear it like a crown of dandelions?

Will it dance if we haul it from the dark hold of a ship?
Will it ring under the chisel when we break its neck like a mechanical snake?

No. But it works.
The word comes down like acid rain
from Washington, and Moscow, and Peking:
the same, old, ignorant lies
for which we'll feed young bodies
and maybe this whole planet to the flies.

14. Pub Talk

"You can't have a sense of community
when everyone's out for themselves."
Leonard smiles. "It's worse than that.
Those who are out for each other
get screwed and robbed and laughed at.
It's this thing we have, this paranoid ethic,
good, better, best, bust! But until
we can see each other
through, we'll be stuck
here, each greedy darkness
lit by dreams of escape."

Our resident cynic sneers, "Everything
runs on the energy we create
in the pursuit of cash. Turn that off
and the carnival grinds to a standstill."
Now it's Helen's turn to steer the future.
"Yeah, people act like if you get rich
enough you never die. But money
can only buy power, man, and power's just
a substitute for guts. Look,
every job that really needs doing
has the same value, slinging hash
or running a corporation, a country,
because whatever you do uses up some
of your life. It's gotta be equal
pay for equal time. And we all
decide what needs to be done."

Honey snorts, "Dreamer! You think
you can get there by asking pretty please?
Those who grunt and squeal at the top
of this garbage heap are junkies.
They couldn't breathe without their fix
of Cartier watches, limos, all that
shit. It will take a revolution, blood
in the subways and waiting rooms."

"Maybe you're right." It's Valerie, thoughtful.
"But blowing up department stores
and banks is kid stuff. We've got to put
millions into the streets, the offices,
universities, courts, bureaus and ministries,
with make-up and haircuts and attaché cases
and uniforms, till we can pull the plug,
every upper echelon pig
burned on the same day all over this planet.
Then we go on TV,
dissolve governments,
pool the world's resources
and begin the long slide back
toward fat and corruption: thugs
in high places, shooting up class
and telling everybody what to think."

T-bone lights a joint, passes it.
His jacket reads, "There's Hope
in Dope." He's really amused. "Fuck it,
guys, just Fuck it. In a thousand years
we'll be immortal or we'll all be dead."

He's got a point. If we can survive
the secret experiments
of Pharmaceutical Giants,
National Defence and Counter-
intelligence, lawyers, gurus, drums
of nerve-gas rusting on the floor
of the Atlantic, caverns of nuclear waste,
flags on the moon, hustle and hype,
and the cold war between men and women

we might learn how to live
without those things we've come to depend on:
drugs, lies, thievery, murder, war.

I walk out into the sun.
It's always been true.
Bare necessities can support
the greatest music, the most intense
life. Grandin, brother, eyes
on the sky in the mornings after
we talked the stars to bed
I feel you with me now
I remember the strength in your handshake
and something you said
a few days before they found you
naked, an empty vial on the desk,
your head on your arms
your arms crossed on the Smith-Corona
and all the plugs pulled in the brightening room.

Love everyone and take no shit.

17. In Memoriam

When light thickens
over the low tree line
and the dream of trout dissolves
into a thirst for fire
there is a moment's hesitation
before the avalanche of a night full of stars.

I feel the old rage, my hands
tremble with the loss of friends
shot, committed, or just
sickened so deeply by doublethink
they said to hell with existence.

I came here to clear my head.
For days now I've drifted
lures by the shadow-side of stumps

dropped flies after an hour's silence
from the risen breeze onto a skylit pool.
Nothing. Not a ghost
of the cutthroat's lunge. Nothing
but the deepening shades of autumn
clouds with cobalt linings
and the laketop changing
from slick steel tufted with mist
through a whitecapped rough of gull cries and hunger
to the rippled blood of another Canadian sunset.

I know that, in this country, freedom
is legal (sometimes). But I know too
that the tyranny of the herd, invisible
pressures, agendas, hypocrisy, gossip
can kill more joy than the secret police.

Tonight the scent of leaves on the wind
the coals of a dwindling fire
whiskey measured and taken like a cure
and the bears, rummaging
through some nearly extinct scenario
break into my wardrobe of sociable moves
and eat my masks
as wind licks fog from the face of the lake.

My tribe is worldwide.
We have always found ourselves
in the sadness of absolute music
in the rich breath of another intimate voice.
Our god is no demanding fool
in the rigged sky
but a cadence we live by.

Deep water. Starlit air.
I am a child and father of this roadshow.
I own no one, and every time I learn
that the heart of existence is untranslatable
I think of a city stacked at the edge of the sea.

The Presence of Fire

Sandpipers

When a wave leaves its glassy wake on the shore
they hunt in the drying mirror
completely at home near exploding water.

They've been here a long time.
Their tracks look like ancient cuneiform
records pressed into wet clay.

Their heads and backs are slate blue
like the sea on a stormy day.
Their breasts are foam in sunlight.

On the Street: New Orleans, 1959

I wake up in the dark, hunched
in a doorway, dusted with coal
from the smoke of locomotives.
Shadows crawl into my blood.

Later I lean against the fence
of St. DePaul's Asylum, watching
one high barred window
burn with the comforts of home.

Anima

1

They were all wrong, grandparents,
priests, the neighbours and those who sell
soap or orange juice
by faking beautiful families
in a box with a glass front.

They said you were functional
like a gland I lacked but needed
to walk through stone into the garden.
They said you lived like a riddle of light
between closed thighs, in the smile
of the right woman, floating
through smoke across a crowded room
or wandering under the starless dark
of the suburbs, yearning
for someone like me to find and afford you.

But each time you surfaced
in dreams or in the flesh
though your presence was unmistakable
as juniper or a breeze from the sea
you wore a different name, a different face.

2

My date's roommate
fluttered her eyelids
and there you were, sea-weed
snake-dance in deep light.

My composure wobbled.
My socks itched. How was I
to know she rode with bikers
lived in a mansion
and had recently engaged a U. S. Marine?

It didn't matter.
I came to see her
in that cloistered school
for girls. Evenings
we'd slip away to the river.

And there we sat, barely touching
our eyes drinking each other's eyes
in the October silence.
It was absurd, and awesome.
And cold. I shivered.
You smiled. Then
after the big dance
we made love in the woods
all night. I woke to her smell,
animal blessing mixed
with pine cones, with rotted leaves.
The world had changed and it was morning.

By the following spring she was gone.
I was sick with loss.
It watered my blood. I took
long walks in the mud, the rain
I tried to explain
your visitations and departures.

Later I learned
she answered my letters
but mother had kept them
in a box to heal
my heart. I left
for good. I tried to get back
to you. By the time
I did she had married.

3

Bright as a flower, calm as a stone
your voice was my whole horizon.

It haunted me
like tragedy in a past life
or wind prints in the snow.
I travelled alone, hoping
to meet you by chance in a town somewhere
and all the time you wintered
inside me.
       In the rattling darkness
of freight cars, in pool halls and locker rooms
I kept you from my public self
like tears that brimmed for a sweet song
or moments of excruciating pleasure.
Until a woman whispered, "It's all
right, men are beautiful too."

4

      Sometimes the light goes out in my
head. There are no stars either. Just the cave
shape's thoughtless dark.
      Then the outer world grows magical.
      Your beauty falls like a wet blue fire.
You're standing near me, smiling, or talking, or holding
your hand up to shield your eyes from the sun.
      I want to look at you, for a long time,
but you can't stay. Your life is hectic, like a white war
or some colossal game in which the rules keep changing.
      When you're gone I remember.
      I dreamed you once as a clear shape, like water
rising from a fountain.
      It's spring.
      I'm walking toward the sunset by a lake.

5

Friendship, that resilient
season returns
like the swept light of a comet.
After years, marriages
her voice on the phone…

History is not what we hoped for.
Lost in a traffic jam
of wills with nothing to lose
you speak up for the right to choose
a future in which life could be an adventure
and not this clatter of tin stars.

Your secret opens
slowly. It took so long to see
that she is
what I am in different shoes.

Jennifer Fox

You were born wise but no one noticed.
It was your beauty they loved.
The platinum hair on your tanned wrist
your green lakewater eyes
shone like money in the bank.
But when you painted abstract sonatas
or solved equations in your head
your instructors blinked.
You were steered elsewhere, gently
and for your own good. Then
at twelve, they crowned you
Miss Midwestern City. Your face appeared
in newsprint like a developing legend.
Men courted you in loose platoons
but it felt like an auction. And there
in the front row sat the old man,
glowing with enterprise,
giving advice like a broker
which he backed with dark looks
a belt and a stick. You fought
back, quit modelling, married
a drunk trucker. A year later
it was annulled. You pulled it together
under a stiff white uniform.
Where would it end? Did it matter?
Your refuge was a strip of sand
between horizons of stone and water.
You'd lie there for hours, your skin
absorbing the kiss of fused atoms,
storing that cosmic summer in your head.
Now, after the rumours and the lies
that built up like a pressure mould around you
you make straight A's and drive like a racer.
There are laugh lines at the edges
of your thin lips, your flared animal eyes.
Your hair still burns like brandy in the sun.

Ballerina

Thousands of eyes nest in the dark
but you are alone, wrapped
in your starched bodice and frills
your face, your arms
bleached by the hard light
or bathed in exotic lavenders and blues.

It's what you lived for
perfecting each tough move
in mirrors, in bare lofts
filled with the acid of daylight
and the ghosts of those who sweated and left.

Now, after the varnish and liniment
after the stretching and blisters and heavy sleep
there is nothing left
to think, your mind
leaps, your arms
are wings, you push
off, and a voice
older than language stirs
inside you. It's like
a flicker from dried bark under twigs
the first touch of a goddess
festivals that open in the dark.

Lost in a self that knows itself
only as body time, you burn
through elegant routines
imagined by those who let themselves go
for years, in the landscapes and weather
of orchestras that couldn't live without you.

When someone asks, "What do you do?"
You say, "I dance."

Slash
to Patrick Lane

1

It's what we do, sometimes, blinded
by instinct. In Mexico
bandits will open tires
or throats even, in broad daylight.
For writers, it's typographical
kitsch, like violence/waste...

2

On the Queen Charlotte Islands, on the shore
road to Port Clements, there is the sea
on the right, singing, and the big trees
on the left, lazing in their earned centuries.
As always, I thought, unspoiled.
Until we turned inland, and that apron
of fir, hemlock, cedar along the roadside thinned
to a few hundred yards of new growth,
and after that, over all those miles
of hills and meadows I learned what it meant:
slash: *And gash gold vermillion?* Well, the deer
have multiplied like rabbits, but the eagles
collect in a stand of trees along the north beach.
They will die there. Contemptuous as eagles.

Someone asks, "but what about the law,
the government?" Sold out, child, by greed
and convenience, the sad equations of ego and gelt.
Guilt is what we feel, now, for failing to own
enough. We stand in awe of the Shah, magnates,
Pharaohs witless and needlessly hungry
for *the energy of slaves,* as if that
could protect us from the dark,
as if life were a hoard

of stocks, keys, wardrobes.
Or paper empires that can kill.

      3

You say we are in trouble, meaning the voice
we've honed and strengthened most of our lives
can only be heard or judged as entertainment.
I know. There are those who spent half a century
learning to read the grain of stones. We pay them
to stack cereal boxes, to polish cars. It's nothing
to worry about. When the light slants
through a fringe of evergreens on the coast road
between the new hotels, someone who worked in a market,
a garage, will call in sick, move to a cloth house
and free the shape of music from a rock.
Others will come, leaving, for a while anyway,
their worries, their tedious jobs,
because they've heard that something's happened
up island. And a man will sit on a log with his chin
in his fist. He will go on staring, stubborn,
blunted by hammers and paychecks and whisky,
until it comes to him: that pointless
mass of granite is a she. And he'll stand
then, in a changed
                silence, clear,
but incalculable, like the liquid assets of the sea.

Vermeer

Light falls
at the foot
of a Dutch bridge.

It is morning.
No one comes.

Unfinished Barn

This blond-boned cage of shaved pine
is a found sculpture.

Behind it the trees gossip
and the sun politely touches its high points.
A voice might be saying

> *...the artist's way*
> *of showing where we stand*
> *somewhere between raw nature and pure thought.*
> *(What is a barn but a large head*
> *whose dreams are real animals?)*

Later when the clean shingles
have silvered like the scales of fish
and the timbers sag with the weight of eighty snows
it may revive an aesthetic thrill
deep in the backbone
under the lid of what we were saying
when we passed in our cars
to be nonchalantly taken like a breath
by this heartfelt nuance out of the past.

Threshold

Five spotted yellow leaves
charged with sunlight
ride out the prairie wind.
When I look again, they're gone.

Over late blue snow, what's left
in the stripped elm is the angel hair
of tent-caterpillars, a moonlit vortex
that feels like the death of Snow White.

Feeling Human

Enough.
I drop from the pull
of miles, miles…into hot
skin. Sweat
trickles. It's like
a tropical disease, but this
is health. Bells.
Birds. The sun, clean
as a trumpet and I'm
sinking fast—my heart
my lungs, cantering still—
into a bay of sweet-grass.

Up there, beached
against a reef of cirrus
the half-moon looks like a shell,
a scarred ice-cap holding its own
in the warm stir of a day that has suddenly grown
immense.
              So this is what it means
to age, to lie stretched out
on six feet of earth
face to face with milkweed launch-pads
and the uncut hair of graves.
What did I expect, money? Parades?
I rub wild thyme between my fingers.
It smells like an attic, nights of summer smoke
like citronella, poultices and soap….

I watch the sky's mirage on the water
burr with the first breeze
in weeks. This is the best part
before it all begins again, traffic
and the hustle of downtown shops,
where the mind sprints ahead of the body
and the air is stuffed with dust.

Every morning, for months
I've come here to run
by the lake in misty light
down the same path, further and further.

Soon I will reach the end. I can see it—
a small white gate where the trail stops.

But now I just want to lie in the sun
between two lives, breathing.

Tasting the Dark

Daisies would be nice, here
in the cool extinction of daylight
among the disconnected legs
of tables, a stopped clock, the staggered
profiles of boxes and stacked books.

Or a soft voice, children
crooning over mementoes,
a partner, a face…

But nothing stirs in this crooked gloom
except for the spider, mice
in the walls, and me.
                              The raised window
holds a smoky haze against the first
stars, like an eye dimmed by years
of grief. And there are smells—
dry paint, coaldust, splintery sills…

Down on the street
a woman in a black coat leans
on her cane. The bus is late.
It is always late. She won't sit
on the bench, but sinks
into background shadow as lights blink
on, startling the sunset.

Rumours of Paradise /
Rumours of War

You Are What You Eat

How cozy.
I don't think so.
I think we are what eats
us—an old friend's invisible
morning-after animals
nibbling at his considerable
intelligence, making his hands shake
at the snooker table. Isn't that more
à cout de la vie and worth
our time than the snotty face
in a margarine ad whose logic would make you
a broccoli spear or a sweet
pepper?

Once
in a serene
environment, I sat
in the shadow of a Maguey plant,
nursing a nearly empty bottle
of mescal and became aware
that there was an organized movement
down in the dark seams
of my work pants. Ants
were digging out and transporting
little forgotten treasures of gold
corn meal and such. They are so
bourgeois, you know, they probably don't
know how to just hang out, they probably have to
get something done even when they're away
on vacation. Anyhow, I liked looking down
at their geography because it made me feel
like a god or at least a giant, and I stayed
there in the shade watching them stagger
under heroic loads, their stuttering
caravans chaining into the limitless daze
of a desert/ed afternoon until
my lover arrived in a taxi. We had planned

to meet in town but I was not in good control
of my time and she had to shout
from the road, which I resented.
Nevertheless, it was the first day
of her vacation and no one seemed interested
in sampling her random lust but me so we did
what you can easily imagine. I remember lying
on my back, watching the fan turn
slowly through the heavy air, and thinking
about a perhaps gin and tonic while she worked
herself up to an expertly managed
climax but still remained unsatisfied because
suppose someone had observed this failure
to finish together like a dance team on Reach for the Stars.
"What's wrong," she said, "What's eating you?"
I looked out the window. Gulls
were buzzing the fuzz at the edge of the sand.
I scratched around but couldn't quite feel
where the itch was coming from, though by then
I could see the truth in her face. Whatever it was
that was eating me, I'd become it. Seaweed
maybe, blessed with insect intelligence? I knew
right then I had to fight back. We got dressed
and she piggy-backed me down to the outdoor café
where I drank a couple of Carta Claras
and forced down little pieces of turtle steak
until my blood reversed
itself and I had to go swim in the channel.

Nouvelle Cuisine

Out in the kitchen, the cucumber and chicken-heart
ragù is bubbling quietly as a mud flat
and I'm in the den, immersed in exotic travel
brochures, trying to make myself see what
it might be like to walk in the sun through the start
-ling ruins of Mexico. Would it help me unravel
the primitive glitches that nest in my everyday brain?
Go stir the pot. Sniff it. Think up a name.

At supper, chambered muscles lie in state
blurred by the sheet-lightning of brandy flambée
like a boatload of hearts ripped from the sawed rib-cage
by priests who knew their victims would scream and wake
in the house of the sun. Their books were knotted skeins
of hemp… "It's new," I say, "Linguine Azteca."

from Ars Poetica

1

No one knows how it starts. Or when.
Maybe it's the first awareness
of pleasure. Or need. A print
we bury deep that cultivates an aesthetic
hunger…
            Later, we'll discover
media: Mud. A hollow stem
with insect holes. A tin pot, a guitar.

Now and then, a shock wave
of percussive light warms as it unfolds
patterns we recognize but have not
lived. We go home to our strings,
our wheels, our labours. The feel
of it is in our heads, a shape
that satisfies vacancy. But it's not
in our hands, our fingers, though we keep
some ghostly echo for a while, practising
technique (which is best understood
by its absence). Never
mind. Begin
again. Listen.
            One day it might be raining,
there's nothing to do in the park,
so you pick up your flute, your brush, your notebook
and let yourself wait, staying
out of the way until it's done
and gone.
            A week, a month, sometimes
years later you think of it
fondly and it returns, like a hawk
or a dove and the journey begins.

3

Robert Frost,
I tell you it's harder to play
tennis with the net
down. You have to
use your whole
mind, you have to love
the soul of the game
more than personal glory.

5

Method is the shadow
-analysis nostalgia
swears by. Once, candlelight
and wine in the cold
storage room under sounds
of wind in the pines
and fountains of Rome condensed
my homesick weariness
into words. Now, every sentence
evaporates memories, goes on
in darkness like an organ
of smell at the end
of a fuse.
                    Where
this particular poem
or its incompatible
neighbour comes from and how
they begin, arrive or decay
in the mind, on the page, in books
on the shelf of a lifelong friend
is mysterious still. Nothing
too is shapely and fragrant. The steps
we invented once to climb
out of grief collapse
underfoot, the places
the landmarks, the sure-minded
rhymes, the rhythms, oh

it won't come back
again, that iron animal, that soft
machine. Even the "act
of the mind" cannot distinguish
itself from the desert
places, the flood of dark
laughter, the whisk
of a snowflake in dead leaves.

What shall we make
and for whom and for how
long? Is a better poem
the same as a better
weapon? What is it
for, if not money
or money's ghost, prestige?
And should we go back
to the ways of ancient Greece
where genius could still make
an honest living praising the King?

                7

If the best you can say to yourself
when you're dying is, well
I spent most of my time
making oddly beautiful structures
out of words, texts
that can never be marketed
as programmes for Utopia,
cures for the infinite symptoms of stress
or even as the shoots of a new religion;
if all you can say is, while I was wasting
time there were those who couldn't stop
                                    spilling
milk, beans, classified secrets, innocent blood;
and if
when you begin to feel
okay about those virtues
of omission, the air hums

and blisters and dead relatives
turn their backs on you because
they'd hoped you could have left more of an echo,
more of a blaze in which their names might have shone,
how will you resign yourself
to your place in the history of doubt,
puttering, turning the limited syllables over
and over, discovering
to yourself in a lost voice how "…this
is not quite true, that's not exact
-ly right…" while pelicans
cruise on extended wings
back and forth across invisible borders?

Inventing Nogales

Having a beer
    at The Acropolis
        lounge on Sherbrook
            in Winnipeg, but really

I'm crossing a bridge

    the water-top
    undulates flaked adobe, thunder
    -heads and wealthy
    azure
        (I've never been
    here before but I like
    the name, the music
    drifting from an open window
    under a boiling sky, the way
    time deepens
        (afternoon
    shadows in the broken streets
    where everything I see
    as my life is far
        away (hills
    the colour of wood smoke,
    heat waves melting
    the trees over terra cotta roofs,
    charcoal and roast goat
        in the wind
        that comes off the desert,
        steady and close
        as a blow dryer
        but already losing
        its fever to the first
        few stars, heartbeat
        slow as the stroke
        of a lighthouse, the pull
        of oars, pushing

a body's complex politics through time

    and I want to drink mescal
        again until everything's
        familiar
        patina burns
            away, but I know
            how much it costs, the after
            -math, numberless
            brain cells
            drying over a dull ache,
            the morning, slicing
            like a sheet
            of glass through damp
            sleep…

One more
beer for the road
to Nogales
    where there is pain
    enough, and then some
    joy, a trickle, a thin
        rush at the sight of a woman's hands
        piling shirts, hats, baskets,
            the canvas above her head
            so filled with sun
            it looks like it could burst
                into flame.

Wire Sculpture

She steps through the doorway,
and curtain strings of obsidian beadwork
rearrange themselves like iron filings
in the force field of her slender figure.

She's late. Already the light
has begun to soften
the studio's white vehemence, the hard
shadows of January elms.

He sits at the drafting table.
Behind him the floor is a chaos
of discarded sketches
and black extension cords.
He nods but does not speak.
She moves to the stereo
touches a power tab
and invisible strings brighten the air
with a harpsichord sonata.

In the cleared space at the centre
of the room, she loosens
her shoulder straps
and lets the cream shift slide
into a wreath of shaded folds at her feet.

He watches her move, pliant
and lyrical, against the hardwood
floor's ruled page, and the tip
of his pen grazes the paper
building a supple concordance
like strands of hair adrift in a stream.

He works through the night.
The blue star of his torch
bursts, again and again,
into a fountain of prickly sparks

until the obscure circuits,
the sinuous lines of force,
are fused, and flow
through nodes of dying fire.

Cooled on a walnut pedestal
it looks as though the body's music,
the dancer and the dance,
have been stilled forever
in a complex cage of air
but that fugue of intimate tensions
will revive and go on
through beautiful changes
if we should happen to walk around it
or turn it with our fingers in the sun.

Dancing in the Mirror
for Annette

1

It's what you do to keep
your dream self apart
from critical paths, paper

clips, charts
and performance appraisals.
After work in the dark

you perform: *battement, arabesque, fouetté
en tournant*...to applause your heart
can rise from, though you know such things remain

theoretical. And while you dream, grown
-ups grow more the same
each day. Of course, the telephone

helps, but those few you could say
anything to, those you have known
for years keep slipping away

into marriages, or solitudes of their own.
Alone: a relentless bell, crêpes
suzette and coffee, rooftop sunsets, stone

-ware and magazine photographs taped
to the fridge: rainbow decals: tricks
of light: house plants: albums: drapes:

then a weekend of concerts and casual sex.

2

Drunk shouts from the street melt
into sleep, and the dim, sleek
shapes cruise and cruise and strike
and you kick back through the bell
-buoy heart's red wash and break
out of breath, into dust,
into a clutter of old
clothes, old books. Slowly
you begin to trust
your ears: the ticking
snow, far-off echo-y
tires on wet streets, the sadness
of time. And there's no one to kiss
you to sleep again, so
you hug your pillow
hard to the hollow
undertow that aches and leaves
you weak, knees
to your chin
your eyes pinched
against the corrosive light
that fades a sea-blue sky to white

3

ashes in the wind. You try to burrow
back under a spell
of soft inventions, but spurs

of punctual, actual day
have already started to press
in around your Japanese window shade.

Sparrows accelerate their helter-skelter
chatter and voices trapped inside
the wall seem to give off the practical smell

of coffee. From a snug wrap
of cottons and body-heat you slide
into the chill. Holding back

a bit, you spin
silent music out into trembling ferns
in warm rain at the edge of a lake, while thin

veils ignite and burn
the city behind you. Your skin
breathes and glows. You turn

everything off but the world
of blocked and reversed
light where the long rope of your hair, your curved

arms and smooth
legs race through a storm. Snowflakes
collect on the roof. Soon

you will have to choose
a disguise for the workplace.
One last kick and you come to rest, ease

your hair into a knot,
your thighs into loose denim.
Blouse. Knee socks. Hiking

boots. And your heart
adjusts to the throb
of stuck traffic. As you cross

the bridge, beautiful moves
inside your office outfit keep you
warm as those breakfasts of intimate silence

we share so rarely now,
and a thousand miles away I remember
how your grey-green eyes

dawned under cover of dusk in the park
that evening you teased
your kite from the shadows

of trees, higher
                and higher,
a wanderer tuned

by love to the changing sky.

Blame

I thought we had learned
how to dissolve
self-importance into the sky
or the calm reach of a lake,
how to leave
some chaos in the shadows
of our lives. Why
stir up that pit
of reptile passion coiled
at the base of the brain?
Can it really matter
so much who
is at fault for the loss
of an address, the missed
appointment, the phone
call that should have been
returned, the broken
plate, the careless edge
of a phrase? Consider
this: when snow collects
in the apple tree
do we believe it will stay
forever? And when that frail
arrangement disintegrates
in a soft buffet of wind,
leaving so many branches
bare, do we try to change
or punish the air? You say
that letting things go
creates distance,
and distance is not love.
Not love, no, but the gap
love jumps to burn
at the heart of a storm.

*Even*ing Out

Last night we drank wine. I
talked about music and you

listened. This afternoon, you
convinced me

to drive north, for the harbour,
the big sky and the sea.

Years ago, you wanted me
more than I

wanted you. Then you
left, and I wanted you

more than you wanted me.
Now, we

stand among hulls
and spars

close
but apart

watching the sun
pour through healthy clouds.

All through dinner, you
talk about painting and I

watch patterns rise
out of chaos. As the light dies

we walk on the sand
and look out over the water

where atmospheres
thrive in a timeless balance:

to the west, a furrow of soft fire,
to the east a night full of stars.

Pas de Deux

He's drinking a Heineken, straight
from the bottle, waiting
for a plane.
              Across the bar
a snubnosed youth machine smiles
an imperial smile over her caesar.
All she wants is to fill for a while
the wrinkled organ asleep inside
his pants.
              He stares back. He can't
help imagining how his tongue, already
chemically dead from too many Rothman's
would taste if it gently insinuated
the tip of itself into the salty scratch
and slide of her pubes, and his eyes flicker
a bit, but his cock continues to
hibernate like a stuffed pundit.

She senses and resents its indifference,
irate because how dare this burned out
slime ball in a JC Penny suit
undress her with his eyes and sip
his beer and blow fat smoke rings at her
invincible glamour. She can almost feel
his democratic imagination freely
anointing the tight halo between her tanned
buttocks, then slipping its tongue, inch
by ounce, through the glistening lips
of her cunt. She squirms on the barstool,
snaps her attention away, but when she looks
back she is thrilled by his eyes

which see her now in morning light,
naked after a shower,
drawing white cotton over her thighs
and snugging it into her crotch,
and as he starts to caress

the curve of her ass and the long trough
of back muscle in which her spine
lines up like a caravan of baldheaded monks,

she hears this male voice, laughing
in its throat, saying please, I'll buy you
a microwave, a Porsche, an island off the coast
of Venezuela, a tin banana executed by the hottest
sculptor in Ecuador, if only you'll agree to sit
still while I pump a spurt or two of hot wet
feathers into the only grip you'll ever have
on supply-side economics. It's for your own
good, believe me, you'll think
it's nifty, you have no idea
how it can improve
the taste of clamato and vodka, and now

she's really seeing red, she tosses
her hair, crushes her cigarette
out and her eyes recharge, but he won't

stop, he's into it, and there
she is again, in a soft focus meadow, wearing a blue
straw hat, white gloved hand dreamily fingering
that taut nub of tissue under a flowered skirt
her wrist moving delicately, bumping against the purple
clover blossoms that have already begun to fall
asleep on their short stems, and suddenly he is
overwhelmed by a brutish need to love her forever
as the disembodied voice that likes to keep
these chance encounters from getting out of control
announces his flight, and he stands and heads
without a backward glance, toward the 747
whose thrust will push him up and into and through
immaculate folds that soften the sky.

Staten Island Ferry
July 4, Nineteen Eighty Something
for R. H.

A day like this
comes loose from its year tag.
Whitman would understand.
Or maybe not. It was just
so windy, and The Statue
of Liberty suffered
as though for the first time
in her life, the indignities
of American know-how: scaffolding
from knee to crown
and all the way up the arm that bears
the torch. There were workers
ant-like at their trades
in the smoky sunset. There were gulls
squawking and fighting, picking
tidbits out of the garbage
that boiled in the wake of the fat
slow boat. There were travellers
crowding the rails
with cameras and zoom lenses,
trying to freeze this moment
into their lives. And in spite of the wind
it was hot. The air was heavy.
The bodies of the passengers
were heavy. But I raised
my Pentax and it all
made sense: the sweating African face
under a cotton headdress, his eyes
gold in the waning sun, and beyond
the sleek curve of his cheek, The Lady
of Easy Ideas, drenched
in flame and shadow, more
unapproachable than ever
behind the struts and platforms
of her long overdue
reconstruction. Then someone

jostled my arm and the shutter
snapped, captured
a blurred wing, a faint
star on the soiled horizon.

This Business/of Getting through the Night

Those who sing so arrestingly
about the lonely night are actual
-ly, at this time, asleep
in their expensive beds
while we dream they are singing
for us, that they know
what keeps us awake and away
from our lives which are not
what they should be. Forty-Eight
bars and the prison
of failed love dissolves
in the small hours
where ice ticks
like a stuck valve in the heart
of a streetlight
and the elms are dressed
exactly like that last
goodbye. But when the record
stops there is no comfort,
there is only the sadness of time
that has no voice, apart
from the wind, which does not sleep
even in the expensive beds
of flowers in the park
where we walk sometimes
on nights like these, talking
to ourselves as light comes up
into the tall grey clouds.

I heard a soldier say,

when the reporter asked him why
he was in Honduras, "We can't
have communists running around
loose, doing whatever
they want." He was a freedom
enthusiast, thinking straight
as a death squad. Dumbocracy
surged in his face: youthful
and oddly beautiful in the light
of the canefield whose leaves knew
nothing except how to grow. What
clarity, I thought, how can you
criticize such courageous
obedience? Well, it gags
reality, this mouth without a question
in its head, this fiercely
moral boy scout with a full
clip and a cause, this great
white hope.

          When I was a kid long ago
I heard it on the radio: the Lone
Ranger's handmade bullets whanged
and whizzed, unerringly disarming
the bad guys, who were always just
a split second slower because
they were the bad guys. I even read
a book in which He got shot
and Tonto nursed him
back from the edge of terrible
inactivity, in a house of pine
boughs in the woods. But even after
such an ordeal he would never
shoot anyone in the head
or give a darn how silver fared
on the stock exchange. Independently
wealthy, he could afford

to let the banged up softnoses lie
where they fell, all over the West.
Always, he knew how to right
what was wrong and always he sang, Heigh
Ho Silver, Away. I thought about his horse
a lot, a metal slickness dissolving light
from the muscles and tendons, his mane
a flurry of angel hair, his hooves, *bright
battering sandals* (Hopkins), his nostrils
pink, his breath nearly capable
of discourse.

          I wonder
now, if this young *Newsweek*
hero-to-be in his fresh
fatigues would be interested
in the words that made me
believe the Ranger alone on the wide frontier,
with his grunting sidekick, Tonto
could never be mistaken or unfair
and that he roamed at one time
in the actual past and might have talked
(briefly, of course, in his usual
laconic manner which is not,
alas, my own) with Abraham
Lincoln, or Teddy or one
of the other Capitalized
leaders of the pack. Once you begin
to imagine the bullet's path
and all that might happen
around it, the technology seems
like a miracle. *Inhuman.*
Of the veritable Ocean (Stevens)
of dreamstuff and so
this morally conditioned upright
Son of Sam (the uncle) wants to shoot
his way to the heart of the problem.

        A little town in Texas,
        The Last Picture Show
        black and white, and the wind

sadder and older and emptier even
than static or dead air
on that Atwater-Kent
my grandparents closed
their bouncy conversations
down for, listening
to Roosevelt's funeral
as though it would actually pass
through the living room
while the sun held fire
in paper shades all afternoon...

Soldier, I salute
your commitment. Don't
come home. Get your hand
-les on the problem, force
the red menace to think twice
before it fucks with a cloned
Ranger (charged
as he is with the flap
of stars and striplings).

Interlude: Tonto, your loyalty
was never in question, the shit
work you did without resentment
serving the star of the show.
What a team you were. Historic
antagonists working together
to save the world as we knew it
from bandits and bullies and asshole
views. Never mind
that your kin exploded
with alcohol and smallpox and other
improvements. Forget the politics
of genocide, justice in the land
of the free demands
this tiny concession because
without you, the masked saviour
of banks and ranches and large farms

will suck air and sift
off into the dry canyons,
merely the ghost of a good idea
who can only make white history wash
too late. So.

The next time a camera pokes that cyclops eye
into your lifelong opinions, the ones you had
to memorize instead of learning to think,
don't try to enlighten the world
with your stunted grasp of Poli-Sci.
Just tell it you have a job to do
then look real cool, real sharp, real bad,
and walk off into the sunset.

Misericordia General

for Robert Emmet Finnegan

The window
itself can't change
and I can't move
enough to change
what it shows me:
the soiled brick
wall, part of a white
window frame,
four telephone wires:
consciousness distilled
to the space between
this tireless machine that breathes
for me, and a block
of sheltered lives.

The swamp invades
itself Under scum
and broad pads green
jaws cruise Almost
nothing
remembers how
to breathe

Slippery tongs
grip Suddenly

flesh gives way

A long, slow
slide and I'm

there

My lungs fill and burn

Grand Prairie. I was born
here. Cannonades

of light over the snow
left me hungry for exotic
wars.
          Hard
to believe, after years
in the signal corps
the great pyramid
cells, the horns
of grey matter, anterior
columns and tracts blown
like power-lines and bridges…

Only my eyes move.

At first they brought me
books, turned
pages till I slept.
I blinked messages
like radio code into deep
space. Nothing
got through. I learned
to concentrate on the view.

Today the wall has broken
out in a cold sweat
as though it were ill
as though the whole damn world…

But no. By noon
the bricks are dry.
By dusk they're warm and snug.

>   *I'm lying on a bed*
>   *of brick that stretches*
>   *and curves to the round*
>   *horizon   The sky*
>   *is a glass kiln   Hot*
>   *wind mixed with green*
>   *shadow dyes*
>   *my hospital gown dark*
>   *as a forest   The bricks*

glow Thick
smoke all around
me then the gown bursts
into flame Ashes
float I can't
feel a thing but waves
that melt in the air make
my eyes water and open

to darkness that thins
as the wall returns...

Of course it's not just
a wall; it's earth, pulverized
rock, shaped
by fire and sweat—lore
old as the Chaldees.

    I remember
the mason I worked for once
(the exact mouth, face
baked like a mask of the desert
under a shock of white
hair, the spare
frame, crooked fingers,
eyes bright as a hawk's)
digging his loam in October
letting it powder under the frost
mixing the weathered remains with spring
water, ground chalk, ashes
bone meal, coal dust or dried
seeds pounded to grist, tempering this
to a smooth pug with his feet
culling and kneading each clot
lifting it over his head
slamming it down into the slick
or sanded beechwood mold and stockboard
squaring the top with a wet strike

lugging the raw brick on pallets
up to the drying ground,

laying them in a scintle hack
under straw to cure in the air

stacking up codes in a kiln
he knew he'd have to break
and build and break and build
again, every three years

kindling the fire holes
with twigs and paper
"to drive off water smoke,"
raising the heat with stove logs
then charcoal.
                    Seal the arches
let it cook for a week.

I'd help him draw the cooled stock,
astonished at the way some change
in temper, heat or stack pattern
could produce shades
of red from scarlet to blood
pudding, pinks, browns, ochre, sulphur
buff, orange and grey
to green or woodsmoke blue.
And they weren't just bricks, but phrases
of a composition he kept
in his head, some chimney, garden walk
or fireplace or gateway
and maybe, if the client could pay
a glazed puzzle that would resolve
itself into emblems, a coat
of arms, a dignified profile, scenes
from daily life.
                    He worked
all over the world, and worked on the day
he died at ninety-four: single
withe, cavity walls, header
and stretcher, spreading the beds,
furrowing and parging, buttering ends,
keeping the plumb line straight
to the rim of the course,

raking or beading or tuck pointing.

English bond, Flemish bond
running bond and cross bond
garden wall and herringbone and Sussex
noggings and surrounds
pillars, arches and quoins
(I studied this, there
in the war) strapwork
gaugework, dentil sets
and rusticated patterns.

Out in the high sun
finishing a patio or pool, tap tap
tap, and the brick, fieldstone
flagstone, tile, would crack
a perfect closer.

     Night   The siren
     gives up its pewter
     ghost   Time
     is a glass shock
     wave that evaporates
     nerve ends   *The first*
     mortar explodes
     the dark like a brimstone
     flower   I'm over
     the hill at last but the same
     habits cry
     the dragon back
     from her peace   Reeds
     now, hollow
     music. Whatever
     it touches bleeds. "I'm flying
     without support ahead
     of the storm   There are no
     thresholds   Everything
     is now"
         This
     is what we were taught
     to fear, this play

of self in the snow
taste of remembered
mornings, in the long
dark, empty of almost
anyone else, but it
sings, this way
of touching the near
silence where all
the mind can reach
and become and allow
to fade fills
even a desolate
street with spring
light that slowly
explodes my cropped
view of the world

From the top right hand
corner, telephone lines
like an empty musical
staff, drape down
and away

> *electron streams*
> *vowels and voice*
> *colours blurred*
> *to a hum*

where birds come
to rest. Somewhere
they have nests and futures.

This time
it's a grackle, ugly
eyes, feathers glistening
like Texas crude, the beak
opens and I hear, inside,
the sound of a stone
breaking, like the cracked note
of the bugle that played taps
at Arlington for J.F.K.

Life has these necessary
flaws that say don't
gloat, each triumph
is shadowed by invisible failures
all of them real, though disguised
by ritual observance.

  Sunfoil flashes
  Aerosol Aerosol Aerosol

  Backpacks and party girls
  Police out on the roads

 Courage, old heart.
 Somewhere in this
 paradigm, the lion sleeps.

I had lost count
of the days, the nights, jars
of glucose hung like sterilized
fruit. Could I have
known how immeasurable
sleep would be
redeemed by bricks? Like faces
in a stadium they look
the same but have their own
wrinkles and weather
marks, the white
stain of efflorescence,
some of them edged
by years of soot
to formal death
letters—diverse
histories, none
of them perfectly true.

  Cockle shells
  Cockle shells

  To warm the heart?

No. The sea
after all,
is cold. Deep
fissures in a
thunderhead. I should
have been that.

Sometimes (in dreams?
I can't always recognize
that shift out of every
-day) bricks
burn and pulse like blood
cells, their ember
flare darkening
at dusk when part
of the window frame ignites
and glows, yellow
through soft curtains.

I have imagined
a woman in that room, singing
her name to myself,
watching her intelligent eyes
in conversation. Soon, we will touch.
Our skins will heat and cool in the dark.
There will be children
and friends whose lives
bind ours to the world.

          (I know that's not true
          or perfect. I know the film
          that keeps insight
          from outlook, but why
          should I care? Death
          itself can only hurt
          as much as a drawn
          shade. I've got
          what many say
          they want:

no worries, no pain
no one to fight with
no one to blame
 and nothing left
 to account for.)

Though I can't see
the sun, I can watch
its moods, modes
and seasons, the day
changing—fierce or soft
with mist—rain, leaves
loose in the wind, shadows
of smoke opening, a gull's
keen glide, the snow
arriving, straight
or swirled, ice
that shines and runs.

 A white horse gallops
 across the field
 into a still
 cloud, and the west
 blue rings like an anvil.

Here, there is time
to dream a new life
before death, before
the 'copters bursting in air,
the sudden drill
of pain in my head
the mud, the lasting silence.

New Poems

The Return

1

By the time he arrives it's too late, too cold.
The wind comes up and strafes the leaves with rain.

2

He can't reach the source, that cave
inside, which is empty, except
for the imminent onset
                    of music….

How did he find it then, in the dream
time, so often and with such
ease? Where did he lose
                        the trail, the map, and when
did the method slur into trivia, fire-fly
                            attributes that die
into silence. Memory fails. Words fail.
Even desire cools and cracks. The mind
is an event
            horizon, a time
lapse blur of old habits, dusty roads and storm
light, far off, promising more
interesting weather, but nothing he hasn't seen
before, an arcade run of bells and flashes.

3

Uncertainty is a principle so deep it's all
that's left of confidence, and the song
he feels closest to, on the stereo
as times rush
                by is *mildly grieving* (Helen
Vendler, on the poems of Charles Wright) and sweet
with yesterday's faith in tomorrow.

4

From the locked crash
                    of dreams, *eternal*
delight seeps back through small disasters
and the spirit, which tends to expand
in crisis, leaps
                 beyond the body's hopeful
distortions. Light
              breaks
                       under heart-shaped leaves
where clusters of elfin flowerets open, purple
and white and lavender, burning
invisible incense, a sharp, sweet musk
that changes everyday air into spells
of memory or desire. Summer
approaches again, entirely fresh, mysterious
but also what it has always been,
that season of freedom and growth he discovered in childhood.

The knowledge that this might be the last
or one of the last fields of time
he'll ever adventure through is no longer bitter
or sad. It's the first day
of the rest of his life
                  again, and although
that magical phrase has shrunk to a knot in his chest
it can still open, heavy with rain, with loss,
                       and release
a spray of tiny candles in the wind.

Summer Night Veranda
to Annette (on vacation in Toronto)

Through a screen dusted with inside light
above clay pots of thyme and coriander and sorrel
the front hedge is an inkblot, an absence
(except when cars pass on the street, scattering
red and white and amber
fireflies through dense leaves).
Beyond it the neighbourhood sleeps.

In front of the pink bungalow, backlit
by a high globe in the back lane, a fir
sags, shaggy and black as a wilderness
exile. Behind it, to the left, a loose
cliff of softwood leaves hiss
in the breeze, washed by the same light
that soaks dry stucco and fills the eaves
of a dormer with shadow dust.

Brisk air cools the sunburned skin
under my eyes. It carries
the flimsy echos of night birds and far off
traffic, odours of wet grass, the river's
breath, exhaust fumes and the spice
of cedar from a rain-soaked deck. Sometimes
a motorcycle starting up, or a voice, or a rash
of voices, or a scrap of music from an open car
window stirs the silence. Sometimes a jet
sails its cluster of lights over the trees
and now a siren stretches thin and breaks
into quick echos, then fades and revives and fades
again, into the diesel blast
of a train but mostly it's quiet.

Split, stacked birch against the wall,
the ripple patterns of light through rattan
lampshades and the geraniums
blooming on leggy stems in their rough peat pots
compose the kind of sweetness travellers catch

a glimpse of as they pass in the night
and maybe hunger after. What do I hunger after
beyond this comfortable house I've wrapped myself up in
as though it could protect me from the dark?

On the scarred oak table you started to strip
last Fall, a cheap straw hat
I bought on the road the year I went home
to help my mother die, stands
in the soft light, its crown
splintered, its brim stained with sweat.

I promised not to miss you, but I do.

Basilico

1

Three plants
in one styrofoam cup.
A gift from a friend.

Their smell dissolves
the afternoon, brings back
my grandfather's garden. Sunday

and *pomidoro* sauce in a cast iron pot,
guests arriving in old cars from the city
soft nights, mandolins and laughter

under the window where I fought
off sleep, then rode
my mother's clear soprano into dreams.

2

Something's wrong. Flooded
with sun on the windowsill, their leaves
go brown at the edges.

I drench them with mist
and sing to them in southern Italian
but it does no good. They suffer

as we do from too much
togetherness. I pull away
the puffed-rice cup, crumble

the earth ball and tug their nest
of roots apart. It sounds
like thin stitches ripping.

3

In their new pots, they have the look
of radical exiles, resentful
and sullen. I put them out

in the spring sun to heal. All evening
at the concert hall, *Le Ballet Jazz*
erases their claim on my heart

until I wake in the dark and feel them
wilting under a late frost.
I go out on bare feet and retrieve them.

4

All day I set them in different windows
following the sun, watching
the light arrange new moods

for the house. When evening comes
I spray their limp
dishevelled leaves and give them

up to the dark.
                    Awake
with the first light, I'm surprised
and happy to see their pumped up leaves

drinking the dawn. I decide
to celebrate, pour a cold beer
into the tall green glass

I found in my mother's cupboard
after she died. I hold it up
to the window, watch

the bubbles rise and bolt
it back. A warm jolt spreads
from my stomach up to my brain

and it's only then that I notice
how their stems lean
over, trying to sleep. So I push

a pair of stained chopsticks
into the soil and tie their heads
up straight. But when I pull

back to admire my work, the edge
of my hand brushes the glass
and it falls to the floor. The sound

it makes as it shatters trips
the same stab of panic I had
to control as a child whenever she left

the house. I see her perched on a stool
at the stove in her small kitchen, drained
by cancer, cooking the last

meals of her life. I bend
and sweep up the curved shards, green
as my birthstone, brokenly

musical as they slide
from the dustpan into the trash.
The room fills with more and more light

and it all comes close again. Her wisdom.
Her temper. Her cuisine. No one
has ever got her tomato sauce right

though she gave us her secret freely:
Five or more leaves of fresh basil.
Half an afternoon at moderate heat.

Grief

How can we tell the light of dead stars
from the light of stars that are still
alive but matured to a phase we can glimpse
only in the script of dense mathematics?

It's like thinking of someone you haven't
thought about for years, and remembering
suddenly, that yes, how could I have
forgotten, this person is dead. And when
you remember, again, that odd habit of
tilting the head when lighting a roll-
your-own, or the little grin and cough
it has exactly the same intensity
as the memory you had before
you became aware of that remote shift
into the vast category of one who is
not with us, and this memory is
as intensely clear as the memory of other
friends you haven't seen for a long time,
or thought of, though they are still...alive...
somewhere...; lucid, even, as the pictures
you have of those you may have kissed goodbye
this morning or argued with last week. They
come back with the same vividness
as the world you perceive as you go
about your life. These different moments
lighting up in the mind are the same, but grief
begins when we want to call or talk or have
good times but no, we can't, they're gone, even though
when we think of them the light in which
they walk or speak or play or smile is the same
light that surrounds the living. When
we realize this, there is a flutter
of distraction, a spurt of panic because
we suddenly believe we haven't worked hard
enough or been thoughtful enough or spent enough
time with those we take for granted because

it is comfortable to assume, with no basis
at all, that they will always be there to help
create those occasions, those photographs, those
little islands of incandescent happiness we'll
need later on, nights when we've let ourselves
drift all at once and much too deeply away
into a groundless absence we suddenly fear
even though at the time we are stroked and
encouraged by the wine-scented breeze, the whispery
leaves we remember, lucidly: a countryside
of October maples whose resplendent farewells
can't help us now, as our lungs feel the edge
of frost and we turn back to the path we can
dimly perceive between shrubs and rocks, a vague
but believable outset that will lead us home
if we really want to go, and we don't know
about that, as our breath whitens and disappears
under a suddenly clear and glorious night.

Aging in the Force Field of Dali's Melted Clocks

Among sparse clouds, flying
east I watch a disk
of light on the upholstered seatback stretch
out of shape and darken too
quickly from gold
to syrupy, coppery dusk.

Over the desolate landscape
a crow like a dwindling jet
shadow lags and lags
until it's a speck among the shards
of a splintered sunset.

Ground zero...glass...a clear
view to the horizon...a tree
like the loose end
of a nerve that's begun
to unravel over the blue
ashes of winter and I'm
alone in the schoolroom where dried
insects glow on a tray...a white
storm is blowing up
from the clap of black
erasers...hunters
lose their way...a nameless
animal curls to sleep
in the drifts...calcium
collects in creased
knuckles...the hair
on my wrist is grey.

Tone Poem

1

Moonlight.
Scratchy trees.
The owls unfold
feathery ashes
and rise on slow big wings.

A witch curdles milk
in a pail. A still runs dry.
A mackinaw full of bones hangs
from clothes-line over a well.

2

Blue nainsook, jaconet and lawn
batiste in yellow, white mulls
violet marquisette, apple-green silk
crimson madras and voile, ballooning
in a stream. One by one
they are lifted, folded and wrung
by the slender woman dressed
in a brace of droplets. Pockets
of trapped air twist, gush
and water like sweet juice
foams over knuckle and wrist.

It's the witch
without her disguises—
dayclothes draped over low shrubs
like a rainbow spread out to dry.

Later, under the trellis
there will be shrimp, wine
and sleep in a loose print
of grape-leaf shadow.

3

When slant light
crosses her dream
she wakes to a feather
touched by the sun
floating over the trees.

4

Evening begins. Lights
in the valley. Calls and cries.

The tramp with the broken
hat, the witch—a wisp
of black smoke in his arms—
turn and glide like night-birds
to the bodiless laughter
of water, through mist
touched gold by the moon
in the cleft sea
of hemlock and fir
down the empty highway.

Star Chant Against Extinction
for Mike Olito

Soon the calling must begin.

Always in this hour, the beauty
of dying light revives
our fear. Birds come in
from the sky as the wind
backs into silence.

If our voices fail
to raise the shining tribes
of the sky, earth
will blacken
and sink into endless night.

We can already hear
the pale ones, gathering
beyond the sacred well.

We set out the circle
of painted stones and begin
with drums and shells and rattles
even before the last fire

dies into smoke and rust at the edge of the sky.

The Final Stage of a Career without Hands
for Catherine Hunter

A fuzzy half-moon hangs from the bruised night.
It looks as though it has become infected
with a delicate mould, a white fungus, tenacious
as angelhair. It has lost its place
in the old stories—Astarte, Nanna,
Hsi-wang-mu, or the Mexican Trickster
Conejo—and must be content, now
with its role as pock-marked veteran
of obscure plagues and wars, the unearthly
darkness packed like grease
around a bearing that won't hold up much longer.

The Gift
for Carol Shields

There is a trace in the wind,
                of music,
                        a voice
we've heard before, not often, this
intimate echo of everything we have
                     always
loved about ourselves—courage, intelligence,
the sweetness of everyday moments that change
drudgery to romance and abundance.
                          Whose
light do we inhabit when a rift in the grey
film of what is familiar opens
and we recover
                that mix of joy and bearable pain
we knew in those flights
                of living
all the way up when we were small
and our minds were infinite? Sometimes
when we stand beside
                  ourselves,
with doubt, bewilderment, grief,
the ancient, firelit eyes
of storytellers bring us back
to the selves we have nearly forgotten,
to the first notes of a song,
or the rich, salt breath of the sea, the moon
shining, its map of blue shadow
not the face of a man, or a woman,
but a deep impression left in the snow
by a beautiful animal, graceful
and so quick it can outrun
thought,
        time,
              and the dull thud of recurrence
like the voice of a great writer: an imprint,
a trace in the mind,
             of what we are
and what we might become.

Untitled

Imagine yourself afloat, in a calm
                              lake
with gulls climbing the haze,
the evening
              sun beginning to sink
behind the fountain-crown of the willow,
filling in windows and bare spots on the lawn
of the yellow cottage with mauve
shadow, and how the view breaks
                              into flecks
and flakes under the light breeze
that sweeps across the water.
                        Imagine
that the nearly red sun in the tree
is too high and too far left. Move
your hands, or your feet, breathe
slowly and wait but do not relax
your attention.
              It's easy to miss,
that one moment in which the scene is complete,
as though in the brushwork of Manet
or Vermeer, there, just before
the force of its coming together
                        pulls it apart.

Post Mortem

Death has conferred a glitzy status
on famous painters who knew their pain
came with the occupation, gratis
like hot silver lining the brain.

Art was its own reward, rain
snow, blossom and bronze leaf
long. Still, they went mad, or chains
of command made sure they came to grief.

Today a Van Gogh changes
hands for twenty-six million. Status
-ticians cheer. A teacher stresses
the investment aspect. But the moon wanes
from goddess to head stone. A state
of the art space-bus explodes in the sky.

Popular Crime

The first must is a preferred lifestyle:
cop or serial killer; soldier, lawyer, thief.
Then, of course, there's the plot, twisted
by things who in their right mind
would be stupid enough to leave
undone, even in thoughtless extremity and yet
we turn page after page, expecting
the chase, the race against time, the hero
blundering through slush ruts, following
dead end leads, frequenting after-hour
fire escapes, badly lit alleys and clubs
while the villains outsmart everyone, break
bones, and take what they please
until we desire nothing
but vengeance, pure as distilled
adrenaline, pumping up veins at the sides
of our heads, as we read on, wanting to burst
civilized habits, losing our trust in the just
nature of things, and this is what we pay for,
the ending ordained but never quite
violent enough, and we're left
unsatisfied, ready to storm the malls,
cruising the shelves, skimming the backs
of paper books for stories no one will write
or publish, in which, when the hero's child
is threatened, he simply breaks
the wise guy's neck, and when the thug
is karate chopped, his gun
is not left so conveniently close
to his fist he has to recover
and wave it around with a grin. The hostage
held at knife point faints when the detective,
who has spent five hours a week
on the firing range for sixteen years
is told to lay down his weapon but shoots
the terrorist neatly between his black rat's eyes.

When the skel tells the witness
I know where your girlfriend works
where your grandmother drinks
where your daughter plays field hockey
the unwritten hero would answer yes
but you're two feet away from the barrel
of the 9 mm. Glock in my jacket pocket
and I'll splinter most of your bones
unless you turn over all corporate assets
and beg forgiveness on your knees
with an appropriate amount
of snivelling. Then, when he does,
our hero beats him slowly to death
in the shopping mall's glass
elevator, in perfect time
to the splash and rush of the fountain
with the wrench he just bought
to fix the drip in the bathroom sink
that has kept him awake for weeks
and made him irritable, unwilling
to listen to threats, or to bargain
with idiots on this unseasonably
warm November night in a major city.

Bleak Houses

1

They stay inside. They dream
of arctic day all night. Say
there's a chalky fingerprint
on the morning sky: they know
it's the moon but they want someone
to sift it for evidence anyway.

2

Evenings, when the picture
window darkens to a slick
of the room we can't see
through, we squirt
starter fluid into the nest
of kindling and old news
we keep like a primitive
brain in the hearth
and as the roar
fades, shadowy
appetites thicken our blood
our tongues. We drive
ourselves deeper
into the complex
rules of board games
as night breathes
and falls all around us.

3

Ownership is temporary.
Rake the leaves. Burn them.
I once had more

than a hundred songs
but don't know how to think
of my life.

I sit in the lamplight
waiting for another useless
epiphany, sipping

the colours of hunger
danger, forgetfulness—
even the magic of money

pales by comparison
to the patriots
who are changing the world

into a better and more noble
graveyard. Somewhere, a saxophone
explores the abstract geographies of grief.

Freeze

Across the sky,
ragged and swift,
an exodus of dream-stuff:
shadows, white peaks, blossoms, wisps
and rare islands of blue
where the stranded early morning moon
will flare before it dissolves
into smoke.
                I stand in the blowing dawn
breathless, cold
unable to turn away.
It comes on like a spell
of misery. Mist
swarming the houses and bare trees.

By noon, branches rattle
their glass antlers at the sun.
There's a glittering skin
on the statues, the streets
are varnished, the courts
the legislature, locked in a slick daze.

Before this, I was lazy.
Now I walk for miles, thinking
to whom do we owe the favour of such armour?
Even the churches wear stiff coats and glare.

White on White

Snow blowing and drifting
beyond the double-glazed patio doors,
the starched carnation, leaning
from a ceramic eggshell
vase over creased linen, the thin
skin of a cigarette and the chains
of foam in a drained beer glass echo
the shock of my beard, my shirt, the hair
on my wrist, and I remember summer,
a rush of angel wings from the outboard,
the swerve and flash of a fish,
little puffs like phosphate meringue
on the lake top near shore.

In Asia it's the colour of death.
Here it announces purity
in a bridal veil, a lab coat
or celebrates the belief
that everything begins again
each day, false
               dawn a clean page or a blank
check, open to forecasts
and signatures which are valid only
till sunset
burns down to a flurry of moths.

Old Age

Every day for more than fifty years
he has taken his place at that table beside the window
filling and folding squares of pastry dough
into spring rolls. We learn this
from a waitress who looks weary
of answering questions about him, the silver haired
leather-skinned, mummified but still very much alive
ancestor, his crinkled eyes ablaze
with the contentment of a man who has worked hard
to fulfill a single ambition, and found it was not
disappointing. His pace never varies.
Relaxed and alert, his frail frame
has the poise of someone who knows
there's nowhere else he'd rather be
and nothing he'd rather be doing.

He's given the restaurant over
to the fourth daughter of his second son.
What's left is the part he's always enjoyed
the most, a perfected skill, practised
in full view of the trees, the sky and the street,
where he can watch the stars come out
and smile at those who wave
without a break in what he is doing,
in the tune he hums to himself
or the time he keeps with his right foot.

Mikey

Freckles, red hair, a shade
darker than copper in the shade
but bright, almost, as brass
in the sun. I didn't trust
his thin mouth, the way he tried
for an extra buck by acting
as though he hadn't already made
a deal with my partner. Annette
loved him. She took me by the hand
to the window, showed me
how brush-cut and lush
our lawn looked, even around the edges.

That was six years ago. Today,
a Saturday, Annette is reading
The Free Press. *Michael*
Perkins, no photo, dead at nineteen,
not *suddenly,* or *after a long illness*
(she knows the obit codes).
It's him, George, I'm pretty sure
it was a suicide. And I, rational male,
already on the defensive
because I wrote him off as a con, insist,
our Mikey couldn't have been
more than nine then, and that
was what? six years ago? She nods
once, but she has already gone
back to that time, that place,
and I can feel her mind
touching his agile body like a light
breeze, her voice barely a whisper,
he had such fine bones, he could have been older.

A cloud seems to have drifted
between the earth and the sun
but it's just her eyes, changing
from jade to slate grey

as she reminds me
how the friend he brought for company
kept bugging him to skip
the trim, there was a gang
at the mall and who cared
about some stupid grass anyway…

We heard this through an upstairs window,
and when the motor stalled we thought
he'd stopped. We got up from the bed
watched him tugging the starter cable,
it sputtered to life, spurts of blue smoke
in the air like spikes of lilac,
hidden blades nipping the already seed-topped
growth and his friend, whining *let's go, let's go,*
but he kept on, his profile so
adult, intent, around and around
as the wild white-topped lawn shrank
to a small stand of scruff
that blew in the sun like an island
holding its own
between the apple tree and the hedge
until he backed up the mower
and ran it over the last
cowlick.

        Oh Michael, Mikey,
I wish I had talked with you
if only for a few minutes
there on the bright, clipped grass,
that morning when she loved your hair
and you were just thirteen.

Body Time

1

As soon as he learns
                 to walk he starts
to dance. We take him to visit friends and he
disappears
                 into a room where the stereo
shakes, pours out
                 Salsa
                 and that's where we find him,
eyes glowing and focussed
                 but lost
to everything in the world except what comes up
through the floor and in through his ears, driving
his legs to a standing sprint,
his arms out to catch a balancing wind.

2

We're a family taking our time
on this hiking trail around Inverness Falls
when we notice he is no longer with us.

Far away, very small under tall trees,
he gives himself to that by now familiar
                 seizure
of total abandonment. We're puzzled,
we can't figure out what brought this on,
but slowly, under the birdcalls,
the scurry of small animals,
the rush of wind through aspen leaves,
we hear what he hears—maybe
the oldest voice on earth, water
pouring over a drop fault
and foaming around smooth stones.

Winter Light

1

I felt that cold word, age
creak in my ankle bones all morning,
but it's my turn to tie skates
for my son, at the rink, at the school.

I'm late, but I've chosen this winding road
for the elms that close overhead
with a gesture I accept at once
as my own wish to enclose and protect.

Cloud wrack smothers the sun
but rust light through a wrestle of branches
soaks into rough bark, a glow
in the overcast, a patch of remembrance,
not summer, not
                        a recovered pulse,
or the sweet stain of time, passing,
but one of those forgettable moments
in which we glimpse what we once thought
impossible,
                        the music of a dying star,
and I know I never would have cared
so much for things like this
in the barren landscapes of my own desire.

2

Out on the ice, his puffed buff mittens
batter the air for balance,
his body takes the measure of time
in a stretched second. He turns, cuts
across his own undecipherable trail,
accelerates to the crisp edge of wipeout,
a wraith among the more aggressive dancers.

He knows I am there, in the stands,
unremarkable in my shabby coat,
and he carries this knowledge like a goblet
he will not drink himself, and will not spill.

Heartland

All afternoon the snowflakes whirl and fall.
In the park, skaters turn on the scraped mirror
of the duck pond. They are entranced by winter
like figurines trapped in a glass ball.

This is a Christmas card, an icon of safety
and it seems to return each year out of a past
that can still reach us. It speaks for things that last,
like a breathless charm against catastrophe

and those who watch from the road are reassured
by the calm skill, the terse redundancy
that circulates in that time-warped vortex
at the edge of day, near the old stone fort
where forebears dreamed, in our nation's infancy,
that every ill we suffer could be cured.

Solstice

1

Stalactites of ribbed ice hang from the eaves.
A whisky jack sits on a branch, cowlicked
by the shrill wind. He is not dreaming of leaves
or the tall grass that's been cut, bundled and hayricked.

Out on the frozen river, fishermen stare
at their rigs: a line, a bell, a black hole.
The sound that bristles along each wind flare
is loose change dropped into a bowl.

Snow falls like scratched light from an old
film or a shattered mirror. It flashes, drives
them deeper inside, where they clench against the cold.
But their stillness masks an aggressive patience, a desire
to stay awake until the dark arrives,
the darkest night of the year, the dead of winter.

2

It comes clear as the glass bead curtain
of rain dissolves into rinsed light with its riot
of white and crimson tigers under the spurt
-flight of a finch, before he enters the quiet
among drenched leaves, his feather coat slick
as tar and buttercup, while out on the water
boat people emerge from yellow slickers
and cast their lines over the shine of the river
where shades of green and evergreen rehearse
their loose chorales, inviting every manner
of ambient being to reach inside for the burst
of speed that will catch them up with the distant shimmer
of hills, as though mere flesh could rise, then disperse,
through the longest light of the year, into high summer.

Bottle Caps

Late afternoon, the sun still
strong among drowsy shadows.

The roads into town are soft, dry, red
dust spilling in, over the edge of leather
huaraches, and the uphill grade lifts my pulse
until it feels like small adventures
have opened a fresh cadence in my blood.

Below a Coca-Cola billboard
and the canvas lean-to with its velvet shade
children play while their mother sells *refrescos*
and coconuts with straws like striped antennae.

When I duck my head to enter
this brief patch of rest by the side of the road
(barely a room, barely a place at all)
I notice how the ground is paved
with bottle caps, rusting
back to the blood crust of original iron.

In the city where I live my other life,
the cycle of digging and smelting,
of everyday use and decay
                                    breaks
when artifacts like these are hauled away
and buried
                        in smouldering dunes that attract
only the determined
                                    attention of poets and rats.

Out in the sun, the inedible remains
of chickens and mangoes and fish give up
their characteristic scent to the shimmer of heat waves.

The children laugh. They have watched my eyes
glaze off into god knows what

fantasy and they wait for me to remember
where I am, to discover
                              the bright
                                        medallions
of *Sprite* and *Crush*, *Corona* and *Sol*
they have pounded with their small fists
into the dust at my feet.

White teeth in dark faces, their hair blown
by a breeze that can rise without warning
to dark waves that break from the edge of the sky
and scatter
                  thatched shade, tables and chairs and mirrors
to a brief report on the Evening News.

When I was a child we saved them, *Royal Crown*,
Dad's Root Beer and even my Grandfather's gold
Ballantine Ale. We used them to play
sidewalk checkers, poker and war,
or pitched them against a blank wall like pennies.

Suddenly I am in love
                          with time,
with Mexico, this village on the slopes of the Pacific,
its light a slow tide
                          that fades
without memory,
                          into blots and veils of a starry night,
with the fullness of moments like these,
curled inside spontaneous routines, so
soft
     -ly explosive we don't know
how they open or what they might mean.

So Many of Us

Evening arrives with the usual rustle
of silks and straw
                    hats, an easy crowd,
taking the air, clockwise
under the *zocalo*'s canopy of oaks, stirred
by the desire to be
                    where others are, to see
and be seen, without having
                              to exchange personal histories.

                    *   *   *

Sails in the bay, sunset hued,
a tilt field of Japanese paper,
cut to the shape of a wave, that slice
of a circle the wind makes
as it turns, South > South West.

For the moment, at least, I agree
with those who swear that everything's connected,
in metaphor, if not in the mind of god.

                    *   *   *

Out on the roads, dust
                    kicks up
brief twists of rock
                    -red brushwork. Distant
fires
      inch across a field.

Those who could paint
                    scenes like this
have been dead for a hundred years.

                    *   *   *

Who speaks for those who inhabit
not poems or books,
                        but lost photographs and silence,
whose lives have left no trace
on what we invent or remember
                        as history
that hologram
                        of random luminescence?

                *   *   *

A man swings a machete and cuts
                        loose
a flock of red balloons. They leap
apart, and rise until they are small
                        black
stars, freckling
                        the afterlight
of another day without rain.

Trumpets and strings announce them.
Moments later they
                        come down
from the white lace terrace
                        to a street filled with shouts
and hats: the bride, the groom, holding
hands, they are laughing,
                        children
let out of school,
into loose ends and the long daze of summer.

                *   *   *

                Time shrinks
to a flurry
                of insect wings. The moon is trapped
in angelhair again. And there is this
                        airborne
onslaught, a feathery diaspora as the trees give up their seed.

A whole generation, like dry tropical snow, drifts
further and further away, and when the breeze
that carries them gives out,
                              they sink
through soft light into the sea.

Catch and Release

I'm standing alone
in a rowboat, playing
a Cutthroat on a barbless hook
and because I believe its life
is in good hands, I take
my time, take pleasure too,
watching it struggle and run,
a flash of silver, a streak
of red at the end of the line.

Then, from nowhere,
a dark shape glides
         and strikes,
                  tows
the boat with the torque of a diesel
out where the lake bed drops
               from sight,
the oars trailing and creaking
uselessly in their locks,
the bow plowing up sunfoil,
until whatever it is
         lets go,
and as the ripples taper off into silence,
the trout comes up, iridescent
scales torn to pink flesh, kicking
more and more
        weakly but still
trying to swim
        off with a broken back.

Land's End

The overcast thins, brightens, and flowers

I don't know the names of give stray petals up to the freshening breeze,
a migration of butterflies from the esplanade's wood planters down to the

Out on the water, a small boat is chasing a flock of gulls.
They rise and disperse like broken fingerprints,
barking, scolding, settling again further away.

A teenage waitress sweeps around chair legs and under tables
on the deck of a seafood restaurant, collecting dust,
wrappers and cigarette butts into small piles.
When she goes inside for a moment, the wind scatters them.

Sunday. A day without shadows. On Water Street, the Gift
Shops are open but the Bars are closed. Strollers
breathe deeply and stop to scan the harbour
where the tall-masted fishing boats rock at anchor
and the tide climbs a slope of darkened stones.

Then someone points, cries out. Just beyond
where the cove opens into The Bay of Fundy,
slicing a white veil that clings to the sea,
something sleek and slow and huge rises, blows, glides
by like a dream and its one fin lifts, arcs, then slips
back under silvery swells, and even those who have not

seen it collect along whatever edge the sea
affords and squint through the suddenly magical
haze, more awake than they ever thought they'd be
on a morning like this, when nothing much is supposed
to happen, a day of rest, but a day of wonder too, and before long
the great finback and her calf come up again, crease the soft
plane of the shifting, nearly flat, rolling field of the bay, one plume

then another, and we can barely hear it, a burst
hiss, miraculous and common as the cracked tab
of a soft drink but so much more complex though it's only
water mixed with breath from lungs the size of a bedroom,
and because they hardly ever come this close,
they are met with silence. No one bothers to fix this
glimpse on film, or in memory banks, but we feel the weight
of each other's presence, miles and miles along the shore,

and for a brief time we understand without anxiety
how immense it is, how old, this gathering at land's end,
this rising of ancient kindred out of the deep, known to us
because we breathe the same air, drink from the same
source at birth, breed and fade in the same shallow light,
here, where we love the sea for what it provides—beautiful
vistas, difficult work—and all it saves us from drowning in,
our own blind wish for windfall or godsend. Hart Crane wrote,
The bottom of the sea is cruel. True. But its history is our blood.

The Question

I came here to work, and to think.

It is the season of clouds, but not
yet the season of rain. Lots
of thunder and wet threat in the air,
but the soft bricks and slick tiles are dry.

I want to see glass-bead curtains
blur the edges of all that is hard
and straight, I want to see lightning,
the *chubasco* crawling over the hills, spilling
its misty spritz onto the *playa central*,
where a gang of kids with stick legs
are kicking up gritty storms
around a checkered soccer ball.

What life can they expect
to flower out of this intermittent blaze
of sun and cloud, sand
and the sea, the town
scattered like bright parcels
among the rocks that climb out of sight
where the coast range crests
into smoke and the drift of black wings.

I wonder but will never know
what dreams they whisper to each other,
hunched under thunderheads in the shadows of palms,
or gathered around the clear flame of a candle.

I ask myself, what is this feeling
I have of being stuck for too long,
                              halfway
between arriving and moving on,
and I think of my son, Evan,
seven years old, his voice
on the phone, very quiet.

I have one question for you.
        (pause)
When are you coming home?

Angelito Beach

The brown pelican executes
                    a knife-dive, but over-
rotates, hits the water and flops
                    on its back, webbed
feet kicking until it comes up
                    with a wriggling
fish in its beak, lifts
                    and swallows, drifts
on a soft swell and I think it is smiling.

But no, it's just a demeanor
I recognize, a deceptive sense
of safety and well being, a light
doze after dinner, and that's all
there is for a fish-eating bird, day
after day, except for the frenzy of mating.

Is it self-indulgent to envy
such clarity of purpose, this wide-winged
mastery of the air, its tacit aesthetic,
its Olympic swiftness and grit?

I shift in my plastic chair, wave
off a cloud of mosquitos, order
a *Sol*. To have everything
you do designed by instinct, free
of commerce and politics and the shadow
that falls between the thought and the act, need
no longer an unpleasant word, but a burst
of adrenaline; and the idea,
the question of death, unknown
except perhaps in that split
                    instant
between the teeth of some other ocean
predator and the dark.

Are there humans who live this way?

And what would I trade
for the speed at which their time
runs out, for a life
that is one irreversible gesture?

I doubt that even the purest
human-hunters can escape
their own designs, those overlapped
strategies of aggression and guile.

Whatever code the pelican unfolds
as it somersaults from the sky, it's clear
we cannot go there. Where
can we go? What rinsed
simplicities can we hope for,
or are they already with us,
imperatives invisible to reason,
misunderstood as judgement
or choice, our endless
-*ologies*, the -*isms* of gender and race?

There was an artist once, in China, who gave all
his brushes away to the river. After that,
he never touched canvas or paper again,
except with the tips of his fingers,
and always, it is said, with his eyes closed.

PUBLISHED BOOKS

Blood Ties (1972)
Open Country (1976)
Flower and Song (1977)
Ideas of Shelter (1981)
The Presence of Fire (1982)
No Feather, No Ink (Editor, with Kim Dales, 1985)
Four of a Kind (1994)
Rumours of Paradise/Rumours of War (1995)
Five O'Clock Shadows (with Gasparini, Mayne, Plantos and Swede, 1996)